Unconditional Leadership

a principle-centred approach to
developing people, building teams
and maximising results

David Robinson

community links

Community Links works to ensure that all contractors and agents producing our publications use papers of a natural recyclable material made from the wood pulp of trees grown in sustainable forests. The processes of manufacturing conform to all current environmental regulations.

Unconditional Leadership 2nd edition Copyright (c) 2008, David Robinson. First published by Community Links in 2004.

Published by Community Links 2008.

British Library CIP record is available for this publication
Unconditional Leadership   ISBN 978-0-9552889-5-1

Design and print by Sheaf Graphics, Beehive Works, Milton Street, Sheffield S3 7WL

Acknowledgements

I am very grateful to Zurich Financial Services Community Trust, Esmée Fairbairn Charitable Trust, Lloyds TSB Foundation and Tate & Lyle for supporting this book and my work, to Jane Tewson for a characteristically generous foreword, to Paulette Spencer who turned scribbles into a manuscript, and to Richard McKeever who turned a manuscript into a book. There is nothing in this story that hasn't been accomplished with or by others and that I haven't learnt from their teaching or their example. I am particularly grateful for the wisdom, commitment and enthusiasm of my many friends in and around Community Links.

David Robinson

Credits

We have sought permission where necessary for copyright images; other images which we believe are in the public domain have also been used. Please contact the publisher if you believe your copyright has been infringed.

We are very grateful to the many people and organisations that have provided images for use throughout the book.

Terry Baker   A1 Sporting Speakers. www.jimmygreavesofficial.com
Colin Grainger   Newham Recorder. www.newhamrecorder.co.uk
Peat Hoagland   Island Dolphin Care. www.islanddolphincare.org
Suzanne Lloyd and Chuck Johnson   Harold Lloyd Foundation. www.haroldlloyd.com
Brian Radam   British Lawnmower Museum, Southport. www.lawnmowerworld.co.uk
Toby Stokes   (07905 450223)

And to all the Community Links staff and project participants past and present, whose images we have used.

Agency Credits
Page 24: London Express/Hulton Archive/Getty Images
Page 46: John Loengard/Time & Life Pictures/Getty Images
Page 68: Ian Britton/FreeFoto.com Ltd

We are grateful to the Times of India for permission to reprint the editorial on page 77.

Foreword

I FIRST MET DAVID ROBINSON over twenty years ago – what I love about David and Community Links is their unfailing commitment to social change. David leads, he does not rule. David empowers and genuinely listens – he works with, as opposed to gives to. His personal ethics and morals are mirrored in Community Links, a stunning community organisation. This is why it is my greatest pleasure to write the foreword for this book.

Community Links has always shared its learning – a true connector and enabler which genuinely believes that we all have the potential to do great things. Through training programmes, demonstration projects and practical publications the knowledge and experience gained through the practical work on the ground is passed on for others to apply in their own communities. Community Links not only delivers a first-rate service to its local community but also researches and works on the longer-term issues that might ease the need for the most acute services.

I am pleased to learn that Community Links' work – sharing information and experience – has now been scaled up with the development of a unified national team, bringing together publications, training, consultancy, research and policy development work to 'inspire and guide' others across the UK and across the world too. This book on leadership from a voluntary sector point of view marks the start of that increased effort, to share the Community Links' way of doing things learned over the last 26 years.

I welcome the timely publication of this book. We are currently seeing a sharp rise in the number of voluntary sector organisations delivering practical services in partnership with business and government. The need for effective management and leadership amongst voluntary and community organisations will have a direct impact on the quality of service provision – often within communities experiencing multiple disadvantages.

The book is written from the perspective of a charity working alongside the local community to overcome disadvantage. The lessons are not, however, only for those who lead community or voluntary sector organisations; this book has a message for us all.

Jane Tewson

JANE TEWSON has founded and led four of the UK's most innovative charities.

In 1985 Jane set up Charity Projects, an organisation designed to bring charities together to share expertise and resources. Comic Relief (Red Nose Day) was established in 1986 and has now become a national phenomenon. Jane created Pilotlight UK in 1998, connecting unusual combinations of people to find creative ways to achieve social change and push the boundaries of charitable thinking. In 1999, Jane founded TimeBank. TimeBank is a Pilotlight UK project created in close liaison with the BBC, government and business to inspire people to make a personal contribution in their communities through the giving of time.

In March 2000 The Times *newspaper identified Jane as one of the top ten innovators of the 1990s.*

In 2000 Jane moved to Australia where she founded Pilotlight Australia in February 2001.

Contents

Community Links began with a bus, an innovative method of service delivery across the borough of Newham.

Introduction

I HELPED to set up Community Links 30 years ago and was chief executive of the evolving organisation for 25 years before moving to the new position of Senior adviser. In this role I have the opportunity to develop new ideas and support colleagues but without without line management responsibility. It is a good place for reflecting on leadership. Over the last 30 years Community Links has grown from a tiny voluntary project, with a first-year budget of £360, to a £9.5 million agency with more than 180 permanent staff, over 230 sessional and seasonal staff and hundreds of volunteers. We are now working with over 55,000 people each year.

What have we learnt and how could that learning be shared most helpfully with others? I looked at books already available, talked and answered questions at training events and tried to identify the gaps.

There is a great body of academic work on both leadership and management but much of that is too ambitious for the busy practitioner. There is also, apparently, an insatiable appetite for business parables but are they useful? I decided that any addition to the market had to be do-able, honest and visionary.

■ Do-able

Sound leadership needs practical tools. I have concentrated in this collection on ideas and techniques which can be used right away in a wide range of settings.

■ Honest

Leadership books written by practitioners are often a bit like the worst kind of autobiographies. They tend to blank out the failures. I think this is a mistake, partly because we don't believe it anyway – no-one gets it right all the time – and chiefly because we learn so much from trial and error. Watch a toddler learn to walk, a child to ride a bike, an adult to play the piano. This is not, therefore, a story of unalloyed success but a collection of leadership experiences, one life, one organisation, warts'n'all.

> This is not, therefore, a story of unalloyed success but a collection of leadership experiences

■ Visionary

Community Links has never been the kind of organisation that just plods on. We've tried to extend ourselves, to test the limits in both what we do and how we do it. My vision of leadership is consistent with that approach. It is leadership that gets the most out of everything – opportunities, people, ideas, even failures. I call it *Unconditional Leadership*. I thought it would be useful to

combine in one slim and easy book, the real experiences and some challenging, even provocative, ideas about unconditional leadership.

I and my colleagues don't live up to all these ideas all the time. In fact, we probably don't live up to all of them any of the time, partly because we are human and partly because we live in the real world where all sorts of external influences keep interfering. T S Eliot once said that *'Success is relative. It is what we make of the mess we have made of things.'* I don't subscribe to quite such a gloomy view but I do think that good leadership is not about achieving perfection. It is about reflecting upon success and failure, learning from both and endeavouring to improve.

> **At Community Links we deliver practical services in one of the poorest areas in the UK**

At Community Links we deliver practical services in one of the poorest areas in the UK – welfare benefits and housing advice, play-groups, after-school clubs and much more. We share and develop this experience through evidence-based policy contributions and through new projects working at the leading edge of social change. Practical ideas making life easier and better: new thinking, challenging preconceptions and raising the bar. This book adopts the same approach. *'Vision without action'* said Nelson Mandela, *'is merely dreaming. Action with no vision is just passing time. But with vision and action you can change the world'*.

Young people outside the
Canning Town Public Hall,
Community Links'
headquarters building.

Unconditional
Leadership

I HAVE A BOOKCASE which I assembled from a flat pack. It is four months old and already it leans slightly towards the fireplace, although I am not sure why. Generally it is fit for purpose. It keeps my books in order and it looks reasonably neat. At least, it keeps most of them. The gap between the shelves is a standard size so the big books don't fit and the little ones fall over. Unfortunately, the alcove in the wall is slightly bigger than the bookcase so there is an irritating gap on both sides – too small for the hoover but big enough to see the dust gathering. The bookcase has a pine finish which looked quite nice alongside all the other pine finish furniture in the catalogue, but when I look at my friend's bookcase I know in my heart that mine is not a thing of unique and timeless value.

> **Our work at Community Links is based on the belief that we all have the potential to achieve great things**

My friend is a carpenter. His bookcase is sturdy and strong. It has unusual dimensions but it fills the gap between the window and the corner perfectly. His books are all different shapes and sizes but the shelves have been designed to accommodate them all. Every inch of space is fully occupied and I love the way the light from the window reflects off the angle of the sandalwood panel, making the room seem bigger even on a dull day. His bookcase is both functional and attractive. It fulfils a purpose, it draws attention and it enhances the whole room.

My friend and I both built bookcases. I as an operative, he as a craftsman. I read the instructions, he made the rules. I did the job, he maximised the potential.

Maximising potential is the idea that has fascinated me throughout my working life. Our work at Community Links is based on the belief that 'we all have the potential to achieve great things. Some need advice, training or practical support.' We do it by working together – former service users deliver 80% of our frontline services. We work very hard on building partnerships with other organisations – businesses, statutory bodies, other voluntary agencies and on drawing together people with diverse talents and backgrounds. The result is always so much bigger than the sum of the parts.

I don't think we maximise potential, in any field, if we allow ourselves to be constrained by convention. I am not saying that leaders shouldn't learn from the past – we should – or that organisations don't need clear rules and structures – they do. I am saying that if a leader is, as I have suggested, dedicated to achieving continuous improvement, no change or new ideas can be automatically ruled out. They should, of course, be rigorously examined and may then be found to be flawed but we maximise our chances of improvement by opening our minds to new possibilities.

> ...leadership that asks, 'Why not?' and 'What if?', that challenges and stimulates and liberates, that listens and learns and grows ... that realises potential individually and collectively

I recently spent time discussing a particular policy proposal with the senior manager of a large UK government agency. 'Why', I asked, 'wasn't the agency working in this way?' 'Because we never have,' he said. 'Why not now?' 'Because we don't.' His exasperated answer betrayed a 'leadership' style that was wholly conditioned by custom and practice. It stifled initiative; discouraged potential partners; drained energy and enthusiasm; and minimised achievement.

In fact it wasn't, in my book, leadership at all.

I think achievement is maximised in leadership, as in life when the approach is unconditional. I think of the teachers, the colleagues, the friends who have helped me most. They are those who have given me their time unconditionally.

I think of my parents, partner, children, others I have cherished most. They are those who have shared their love with me unconditionally.

And I think of the leaders I most admire; Mahatma Gandhi or Nelson Mandela or a dozen others much closer to home. They are those whose leadership has been rooted in values, unconditionally upheld, but soaring in breadth and vision – Unconditional Leadership

I am frustrated by uniformity, by organisational objectives which limit and condition, by values which are frail and shifting, by structures which cramp and constipate, by people who are diminished and detached, by leadership which is arrogant or fearful or both – leadership that minimises its opportunities, its resources and its potential.

I am interested in ideas which are big enough to change us, as individuals, as organisations, as a wider society (Chapter 2) I want to work with big values that inspire but brook no compromise (Chapter 3) and I am interested in setting objectives which are strong enough to stretch us, to squeeze out every ounce of potential (Chapter 4) and with structures and methods that bring the best out of everybody (Chapter 5) and with people who share my enthusiasm but offer different talents and perspectives (Chapter 6). I've learnt that such relationships only work when they work both ways (*Chapter 7*), that we can learn as much from failure as we can from success (*Chapter 8*) and that effective change is a well paced journey in the company of friends (*Chapter 9*). And finally, because we're all learning all the time, this edition concludes with reflections composed three years after the first edition *(Chapter 11)*. I'm interested in leadership that asks, '*Why not?*' and '*What if?*', that challenges and stimulates and liberates, that listens and learns and grows. Leadership that realises potential individually and collectively.

I am interested in '*Unconditional Leadership*' and it begins where Community Links itself began, with the realisation that whatever our status or our background we all have something different to contribute.

'We all need help at some time in our lives and we all have something to give'.

Community Links' first Annual Report

Unconditional Leadership

A Good Beginning

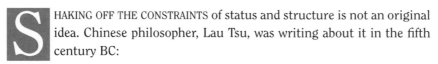

S HAKING OFF THE CONSTRAINTS of status and structure is not an original idea. Chinese philosopher, Lau Tsu, was writing about it in the fifth century BC:

> *'Go with the people, live with them, learn from them, start with what they know, build with what they have. But with the best leaders when the work is done, the task accomplished, people will say "we have done this for ourselves."'*

If it isn't a new idea it is one whose time has come. Simon Caulkin might have been making the case for Unconditional Leadership when he quoted Mercer's Human Resource Consulting in *The Observer* on 6 July 2003. Their research had shown that *'only four in ten employees trusted their managements or thought their behaviour was consistent with company values'* Caulkin wrote:

> *'Whatever the enlightened rhetoric, implicit in the structures, process and cultures of most organisations is the assumption of command and control. Managers decide, others do… Such regimes – often even tougher and cruder in the public than the private sector – are built on secrets and lies … (they) manufacture cynicism and distrust'.*

Leaders who are not constrained by these rigid 'structures, processes and cultures' are free to progress an idea or an organisation not by dragging it forward from a distant edge but by working with others, pushing and pulling together. This doesn't mean that the leader isn't in charge. The leader's role is pivotal but their success is dependent on the commitment of the team, not the subjugation of subordinates. Conditional leaders will think of pyramids and the uppermost tip; unconditional leaders will see the unit as a circle. They will be at the centre, the focal point, passionately immersed in the work, experiencing the aspirations of the team and of their public. They will establish their authority by sharing ownership and responsibility within a clear and reciprocal contract, micro-managing very little but influencing all. They will be at the heart of the enterprise, pumping moral certainty – the life-blood of any movement – not trickling down but flooding out, nourishing, sustaining, growing.

> at the centre, the focal point, passionately immersed in the work

I am a believer in Unconditional Leadership, and I'm trying to be a practitioner. This book is about my discoveries, but I write as a traveller, not an inventor; very little is new. These are the paths I have taken, this is what I've seen and heard, here is what I've learnt.

I don't want to polarise the alternatives. Leadership is an art, not a science. Like conversation, there is no single right way of doing it but there is no doubt that some do it better than others. There is room for a range of approaches, but much of the literature – and apparently, conventional wisdom – still assumes a command-control structure. Perhaps 'feminised' a little, more collaborative and consensual than might have been typical a generation ago, but still clearly driven from the top. I want to discuss leadership from an alternative perspective, not conditioned by convention or constrained by traditional structure.

> Leadership is an art, not a science. Like conversation, there is no single right way of doing it

This isn't an instruction manual. It is a collection of observations from that particular position. The section on objectives, for instance, suggests that they are not a fixed state but rather a continuous process, constantly stretching, stimulating, challenging and inspiring. Values on the other hand are set in stone and are the bedrock on which all else is built. These are the characteristics of unconditional leadership and may not, on paper, look like a particularly radical alternative. But think for a moment about famous organisations in the public eye – commercial, public, political, voluntary. How many actually seem to operate in the opposite mode – apparently unable to risk significant change in their day-to-day work (fixed objectives), but seemingly more flexible on the underpinning ethics (fluid values)?

> **'This collection is…for anyone with an interest in leadership, and I don't just mean people who run organisations'**

In recent years I've heard Tim Smit, Emlyn Hughes and Benjamin Zander talk about leadership. Their backgrounds are diverse – the Eden Project, the England football team, the Boston Philharmonic – and, of course, their stories were very different, but it was the lessons behind the experience which I found valuable. Similarly, this collection is born out of my 26 years at Community Links. It is about the approaches that have worked well for us and about those that haven't. It draws on the principles of community development but it isn't about this organisation or its professional function. It is for anyone with an interest in leadership, and I don't just mean people who run organisations. Leadership is much bigger than that.

It is possible to lead a tiny group within a bigger enterprise; successful entities of any size need many leaders, to lead a movement or community group or voluntary association, to lead the development of an idea. Leaders don't even need followers – at least not in the first place. History is bejewelled with examples of leaders whose ideas were at first regarded as daft or impossible, but who later succeeded. Leadership is not, in my book, an exclusive status. Unconditional leadership is open to us all. It is, after all, as Lighthouse founder Christopher Spence has written:

> **'Leadership is not, in my book, an exclusive status. Unconditional leadership is open to us all'**

'…*our nature to lead – we lead our lives making sure that things go well for us and those about us. We share who we are and what we have. We beautify our environment. We step forward for what we believe in and value. We speak up, to influence, attract, inspire. We tell the truth. We care. We laugh. We dream. These natural expressions of our humanity are in fact the foundations of real leadership*'.

My own background doesn't need to detain us for long – I've only ever done one proper job! However, you should know something about Community Links to understand the context. Appendix 1 explains more but, in brief, we began 30 years ago with two basic principles:

> **Our work is based on the belief that we all have the potential to do great things**

First, we wanted to tackle our local problems. East London was towards the top of most league tables measuring poverty and social exclusion. *Second,* we wanted to involve the whole community in the process. Community Links wouldn't be about social workers or teachers doing things for us or at us, but about enabling, supporting, training local people. After a testing year operating from home we acquired our first permanent centre – a little lock-up shop in East Ham. The late Bette Young – an early volunteer – remembered those days in our 21st Annual Report. We called her contribution a 'good beginning'.

A Good Beginning

'I remember the little shop. It was damp and smelt of coal tar from when the chemist used to be there. There were always boys there, at first three but then more, boys who should have been at school. I know some of them were in trouble but they were always good to me. Some people said it's just for the youngsters, but I said it's for everyone and gradually we got things going. Things that are still going now. Advice and clubs, everything really. I was 65 then. I remember thinking I'd seen a lot of bad things but this is good.

'Of course, Community Links is much bigger now and other people seem to take notice. We've been on the TV and in the paper, people from the government have been down and I said to Prince Charles, 'It's me again' when I saw him last time. But I'm glad people take notice. I know lots of people who've got better lives because of Community Links but I can't believe it's been 30 years. It feels like we're only just beginning'.

Bette Young – an early Community Links volunteer – writing in 1999

Bette led from the middle. She got stuck in, planning and reaching new objectives for Community Links but always rooting her contribution in our founding principles. She wasn't fazed by the fluid structure or by the unconventional company, indeed she saw value in diversity. Bette served on our management committee for 15 years and ran our pensioners' work. She was an unconditional leader.

Thirty years on we now work with more than 50,000 people a year, employing a permanent staff team of 185 and several hundred volunteers. Our work is based on the belief that we all have the potential to do great things. Some need advice, training or practical support. Our activities in East London include education programmes with non-school attenders, family advice sessions, youth work with young people on the street, training schemes, counselling groups, emergency services and much more. We pioneer new ideas and share the learning nationally with demonstration projects, evidence-based policy contributions, training programmes and practical publications. And, as I have said, we do it together – an extensive network of users, volunteers, paid staff, partners in business, government and other organisations.

> '...we do it together – an extensive network of users, volunteers, paid staff and partners'

We endeavour to share what we have done. This publication is the latest example, because although slavish imitation will never change the world, readers can interpret and adapt and through the written word we can both share ideas and keep them at the same time. I have tried to avoid simply recounting successes. Life is far more complicated than that and many of the biggest learning experiences are neither all good nor all bad but a mixture of the two. Take, for instance, our adventure with John Stonehouse, many years ago.

Community Links was a couple of years old when the ex-Postmaster General entered our lives but he had been a big story for a long time. The former government minister had become embroiled in a financial scandal and disappeared in 1974. The hunt for Stonehouse had filled acres of newspaper space until he was finally found and arrested in Australia. In late 1979, towards the end of his subsequent prison sentence it occurred to us that here was an able and well-connected man who needed to rehabilitate himself. Toynbee Hall – a large and successful East London charity – had forged a very productive relationship with John Profumo, another senior politician who had fallen from grace. Might we do the same? A speculative letter led to a couple of improbable meetings and, in short order, a deal was done, JS would work on fundraising and be paid a very modest wage subject to performance.

We had seven members of staff at the time and still operated from the shop. There wasn't space for everyone to have a desk. This was his first culture shock but not the last. I remember staff meetings as a particular challenge for us all. Our new junior colleague sometimes struggled with the dynamics of a senior management team who were all considerably less than half his age.

John went on to raise modest sums over a couple of years. He freely confessed that he'd never done anything so difficult before, but he had found an environment in which he could rebuild his life gently and usefully. We, above all, learnt. Big things – the value of the bold move, for instance. Some potential supporters thought ours was a brilliant strategy and some didn't but we were certainly noticed and talked about, to an extent that would have taken years to achieve through the dogged pursuit of our day-to-day work. And little things – I was particularly impressed by John's balanced approach to failure and success. Whether a benefit night had raised money or flopped miserably he'd still be back at work at 8.15 the next day, neither triumphant nor downcast but quietly, diligently getting on with the next job.

> 'you can't take responsibility for anybody else, or anything else, if you don't first take responsibility for yourself'

Our first press conference was especially memorable. Six weeks after his release from prison the media still hadn't found him. The story had begun to assume the same proportions as the police hunt four years earlier. The 'conference', in the shop and spilling onto the pavement, was barely-controlled mayhem. Next morning every daily paper carried the story, most with pictures. The *Mail* considered Community Links 'so far to the left it is almost toppling off the edge of the world' and the *Telegraph* couldn't bring itself to use my name or title preferring instead to describe the chairman of the conference as 'a bearded young man'.

I learnt professional lessons about the importance of preparing a story, of focusing on a small number of messages, of briefing individuals. And I learnt personal lessons. I remember being particularly struck by JS's composure when the photographers were banging rhythmically on the plate glass window two hours before the event. Whilst I ran around peeping through curtains, re-arranging chairs, skipping lunch and talking to anyone who telephoned, John ignored everybody, enjoying a quiet sandwich with coffee from a thermos flask and a copy of *The Times*.

I was exhausted before the conference began whilst he – the centre of attention – was cool and focused throughout. I learnt that you can't take responsibility for anybody else, or anything else, if you don't first take responsibility for yourself.

Our Value Statement has been particularly important to us at such times. It doesn't matter what other people think or say, what do we believe? If we are clear about the answer to that question we can work out for ourselves what is right or wrong and we can face criticism and controversy with courage and confidence.

Community Links' Value Statement

'To tackle causes not symptoms, find solutions not palliatives. To recognise that we all need to give as well as to receive and to appreciate that those who experience a problem understand it best. To act local but to think global, teach but never stop learning. To distinguish between the diversity that enriches our society and the inequalities that diminish it. To grow – but all to build a network not an empire. To be driven by dreams, judged on delivery. To never do things for people, but to guide and support, to train and enable, to simply inspire.'

communitylinks

'To simply inspire' – lots of people over the years have told me that that is a split infinitive. I expect it is but one of the good things about leadership is that sometimes you can make your own rules. And (there goes another rule) the best bit about Unconditional Leadership is that you don't have to wait until you're a statesman or a general or a captain of industry. Anyone can do it, as we have shown at Community Links, with an example or an idea or just by choosing the path less trod. *'How wonderful it is,'* wrote Anne Frank, *'that nobody need wait a single moment before starting to improve the world.'*

An admiring crowd greet Mahatma Gandhi on his visit to Canning Town in 1933.

London Express/Hulton Archive/Getty Images

Establishing values that push

ON 4 FEBRUARY 1922 a peaceful march reached Chauri Chaura. The people were calling for self-rule in India and were part of the massive civil disobedience movement led by Mahatma Gandhi. Police blocked their path. The marchers lost their patience. They overcame the officers, chased them back to the police station and set fire to the building, killing 22 people.

Mahatma Gandhi was appalled. His movement was peaceful. This was his fundamental value. India had appeared to be on the brink of independence but Gandhi pulled back, suspending the non co-operation movement and saying that the country was not yet ready. For Gandhi the end did not justify the means. The two were inseparable. His position exasperated allies in Congress but now, with the benefit of hindsight historians can see very clearly that Gandhi's moral certainty was not a personal indulgence but was the movement's greatest strength – the source of its influence. He realised that, like any voluntary association, the movement would have been pointless and powerless without an unremitting commitment to fundamental values.

> *...the movement would have been pointless and powerless without an unremitting commitment to fundamental values*

If objectives pull the enterprise towards ever more challenging targets, values push. Successful organisations drive forward from a solid base of absolute moral certainty. Objectives are dynamic, changing over time, but values are unconditional. We don't know exactly what challenges we will face tomorrow, but we do know how we will behave.

Elsewhere in this collection, constant change is embraced as a given, a desirable, almost a necessity in any dynamic organisation. The values are the exception. They are the abiding moral core of the enterprise, constant and enduring.

Community Links began with the objective which was included in our constitution: *'to encourage and enable groups and individuals to understand and to tackle their own problems and those of the wider community'*. That explained what we wanted to do but it didn't say how we would do it, and it was phrased in terms which satisfied the lawyers but were never likely to inspire anybody else. We moved on to a Statement of Purpose which I introduced in the first chapter and which began to lay down the values of the organisation:

> **Our power is derived from our values. Not just our right to lay down internal rules, but also our mandate to lead**

'To generate change. To tackle causes not symptoms, find solutions not palliatives. To recognise that we all need to give as well as to receive and to appreciate that those who experience a problem understand it best. To act local but think global, teach but never stop learning. To distinguish between the diversity that enriches our society and the inequalities that diminish it. To grow – but all to build a network not an empire. To be driven by dreams, judged on delivery. To never do things for people but to guide and support, to train and enable, to simply inspire'.

The statement is not a description of Community Links. It doesn't tell you much about what we do but it does explain how we do it and we tried to use language that would inspire, motivate and, ultimately, unite people of a like mind. We were defining the values on which we would expect to be judged. Thus whilst, for instance, the constitutional objective would have allowed us to support a racist group who argued that they understood and were tackling community problems, our statement of purpose made it clear that we would not. Values are not the same as rules, but rules may flow from them. Our power is derived from our values. Not just our right to lay down internal rules but also our mandate to lead and, in the case of Community Links, to call for policy changes, to seek state funding or to ask for public donations.

Over time, the values need to be seen to work in practice. We recently set ourselves the task of producing a CV for Community Links, which took each of the values in the Statement of Purpose and illustrated them with at least one example from our recent work. The result has become a marketing tool (it is reproduced as Appendix 2) but the process was even more helpful, revealing what we do well and where we had numerous examples to choose from and the priorities for our time in the future.

Strong leadership must be built from a solid foundation. The values provide that bedrock. You can't change the foundations without demolishing the building. Similarly, you cannot change the values of an organisation without destroying its integrity. Mahatma Gandhi was an unconditional leader who understood that maximum strength could be derived from an unflinching commitment to key principles. Although the temptation must, at times, have been almost overwhelming he recognised that placing conditions on fundamental values would ultimately destroy the integrity of the movement he led.

> **Strong leadership must be built from a solid foundation. The values provide that bedrock**

In a successful organisation values are not a pious sentiment filed away with the constitution, but are a practical tool guiding and shaping the day-to-day behaviour that will enable the enterprise to fulfil its potential. These principles are worthless if they are not communicated effectively and if there aren't mechanisms in place for ensuring that they work in every aspect of the organisation. Enron apparently had a code of ethics which ran to so many pages that it was bound into a book. I understand that you can buy it on e-Bay where it is now worth more than it ever was to senior managers of the company.

Enron is now notorious for the unprincipled way in which its leaders ran the business, but it is equally important that staff

|Code|of Ethics

July, 2000

on the frontline understand and implement the values. I recently had cause to complain about a television, the policies of the company that sold it to me and the attitudes of their retail staff. In searching out the head office address I stumbled across their 'vision'. Nothing could have been more remote from my experience as a consumer. Did the staff disagree with the values or simply not know about them? Were they given the resources, the training, the right kind of responsibility to carry through the vision or was the high-flown rhetoric detached from day-to-day reality?

In my vision of unconditional leadership, the values are not the preserve of the hallowed elite but are owned by every member of the enterprise, influencing and informing their routine activity. Such enterprises are invariably better at retaining staff and in attracting the best new recruits, more efficient and more effective. Thus, like so many ideas in this collection, there is both a threat and a promise here. Getting it right isn't just an ethical imperative; it is also in every sense, 'good business'. Getting it wrong is bad business – as some businesses have discovered to their cost.

> **Strong values well considered and well communicated will grow over time, but they won't change**

When British Airways attempted to re-brand themselves with tail fins representing different cultures, they attracted criticism for, amongst

other characteristics of mono-culturalism, their predominately western menus. The company was laying claim to a laudable value but one which was not reflected in the customer experience. Both share price and market share were adversely affected. Perhaps this is because the 'value' wasn't a real one running through the DNA of the organisation, understood and upheld by all its members.

It was, at best, an aspiration; an objective to be pursued. At worst it was a shallow marketing device. Our marketing people can communicate our values but they alone cannot invent them. That is a job for us all.

Unconditional values well considered and well communicated will grow over time, but they won't change. When we talk internally about '*Community Links' way of doing things*', we are not referring to the small print in the staff handbook, we are talking about the values which underpin an attitude, a certain kind of behaviour experienced consistently by all our users throughout the Community Links network. I believe that organisations that act with this kind of unconditional moral certainty demand loyalty, pride and commitment. They may not always be the first off the block, but they will maximise every opportunity and they will, ultimately, achieve the results which will elude their flakier rivals.

'Would you tell me please which way
I ought to go from here?'
'That depends a good deal on where
you want to get to,' said the cat.
'I don't much care where,' said Alice.
'Then it doesn't much matter which
way you go,' said the cat.

Alice in Wonderland, Lewis Carroll

John Teniel's original illustration for Lewis Carroll's children's classic Alice In
Wonderland. He was also political cartoonist for Punch magazine.

Maintaining objectives
that pull

W E KNOW that we can't plan the route until we agree on the destination, but that doesn't necessarily mean that we have to keep going to the same place or down the same road day after day. Unconditional leaders will constantly stretch themselves and their movement with new targets. We often talk about setting objectives as if, once established, they are fixed forever. Unconditional leaders 'maintain' objectives constantly, reviewing and updating. Objectives should pull us forward. They should empower, not constrain; enlarge our imagination, not belittle our purpose; engage, inspire, suffuse all that we do.

The objectives at the heart of my vision of unconditional leadership are a far bigger idea than the soulless list that we can read on corporate websites or the front pages of so many annual reports. They are not just about *what* we do but also about *how* we do it. Not just short-term outputs but also long-term outcomes, and certainly not just a batch of bullet points but a dynamic collection of ideas, continually shaped by new thinking and new experiences.

The objectives should draw us on, spotlighting the purpose of our work and illuminating the process. Establishing them and achieving them is a continuous and essential bodily function in a living organism. It stops and the body dies.

'It is not the strongest of the species that survive, nor the most intelligent but the one most responsive to change.'

Charles Darwin

It is the role of the leader to create a culture in which the objectives influence every action. This responsibility is not unique to those who lead from the middle, but it is especially important. All leaders benefit from winning hearts and minds, but a commitment to shared objectives is essential for those who rely on active engagement rather than on command and control.

To achieve and exploit this central position in the life of the movement the objectives must be clear, effectively communicated and constantly challenging. This can be easy at the beginning when all goals are new goals, but maintaining the pace, avoiding burn-out, building a sustainable movement is far more difficult. After a while comfortable patterns begin to set in, sparky founders start to lose interest and progress slows down... for all but a few.

In every field there are those that take the dotted path. These are the market leaders, the trailblazers, the best. Always with one eye on the goal after next.

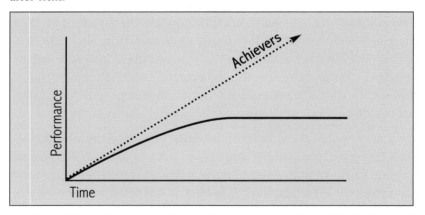

The achievers in every sector are those who have thought widely about every aspect of performance. This cannot be achieved unilaterally or by the top team. Every perspective is important. What might 'excellence' include? Certainly it involves the internal means of production as well as the external products of delivery, but maximisers will encourage thinking beyond these parameters. What is the environment, the physical manifestations of the culture in which the work is developed? How can all this be drawn into the stretching of our targets and, ultimately, the improvement of our performance?

I was taught in classrooms that were plain and functional. My children's schools are full of colour. Educational exhibitions on every wall. I know where I would prefer to learn, indeed where I would prefer to be.

In a maximising environment, everything and everybody communicates the objectives and contributes to their achievement. Starbucks' Chairman, Howard Schultz, has led the development of the coffee shop chain from 11 stores and 100 employees in 1987, to 7,000 stores and 70,000 employees today. His leadership mantra is 'everything matters'. Lighting, music, décor, even smell are all considered and planned.

> **All leaders benefit from winning hearts and minds, but a commitment to shared objectives is essential**

In the early 90's we renovated the derelict Canning Town Public Hall and turned it into a new home for Community Links. We took a clear decision to spend extra effort and extra money on a top quality job. Our neighbourhood in East London is overcrowded and bleak. We wanted to make Canning Town Public Hall a facility which local people could be proud of, the kind of place that just entering the doors would make you feel good. It was a vision which partners could understand and they supported it. Together we achieved exceptional standards of excellence both in the little details and also in the grand design.

Fourteen years on I am still uplifted on sunny days by walking where the light streams through the beautiful renovated stained glass windows. Of course it is lived in now but it is also respected as fine things are, with little deliberate damage and it, in turn, demonstrates our respect for our visitors. We keep a vase of fresh flowers on the Reception desk for the same reason. Their presence says 'We respect you. Please respect us.' The flowers say more about our objectives than 100 printed notices.

On a visit to America, Oscar Wilde was once asked why he thought American society was so violent. *'Because your wallpaper is so ugly,'* the writer replied. All he could see was big buildings and grubby streets. We are all influenced by the environment we inhabit. This is what I mean by the importance of objectives 'suffusing' all that we do. We are all influenced by the view. Unconditional leadership reaches beyond the product and the process and seeks to ensure that the whole environment contributes to, rather than detracts from, the success of the enterprise.

How do we know when we are getting it right? With the short bullet point list at the front of the Annual Report it's relatively easy, but we can't derive simple fixed measurements from the bigger concepts. We have to establish surrogates for success, all-embracing tests which encapsulate the essence of what we are trying to do and the reason why we are trying to do it. Here is one of mine:

For years I could look out of our office window early on a Monday morning, across the market, to the queue outside the Post Office. It wasn't open at that time but already pensioners, single people, mothers with children were waiting for their benefit payment. Our sponsors could take the money that they'd been giving us, convert it all into used fivers and hand out bundles to the people in the queue. It would bring immediate comfort, relief, joy. It could be a worthwhile thing to do. Doing otherwise required Community Links to do better. To make a legitimate case for their money we had to prove that we could add to the value of the fiver and bring greater benefit to the queue. We might be running training, or producing publications or delivering other services remote from the frontline. The distance didn't matter but the lineage was crucial. In the end, the money must have a measurable impact on the proverbial queue and the impact must amount to more than could be achieved with the

straight-forward distribution of the cash. I always found this a revealing and helpful way of thinking about how we prioritised the use of our resources.

I know other organisations and departments have similar tests. The typical user or customer tests are particularly popular. *'What would Henry think?'* The leader challenges the team and because we have created Henry in the form that so perfectly reflects our objectives we know when we are getting it right and where Henry would demand improvement. Essex Man once played the same role for the Conservatives, Mondeo Man and Worcester Woman for the Labour Party.

> **Unconditional leadership seeks to ensure that the whole environment contributes to, rather than detracts from, the success of the enterprise**

Tests like this won't produce a definitive measurement. We can't say we achieved 100% but that in a sense is the point. If our objectives constantly challenge us to move forward there will never be a 100% achievement. Unconditional leadership is not about ticking boxes but about endeavouring to harness every influence, about continuously reaching higher, not about overcoming a single barrier but about going beyond ourselves, pushing out the limits in every direction again and again. Achievement is judged, not measured.

What does all this mean in practice? First we need the shortlist, the bullet points, couched in terms that lead us on. Not a single fixed point on a straight line but aspirations on a spiral, leading us higher and higher, continually stretched and added to.

Then we must look at how we apply them in every aspect of the life of the enterprise. Once planted down in the most improbable places they will continue the process of communication, just as the walls now communicate the objectives of the school, influencing behaviour and helping to shape the next stage of development.

Thus we continue on the upward path, the dotted line. Those simple statistics are just one dimension. When a leader is judging progress, as well as measuring it, they will know that they have created a culture where the objectives have moved off the written page and assumed many dimensions at the centre of the real day-to-day life of the enterprise. Now the objectives, as much as the leader, are leading from the middle, maximising potential in every nook and cranny.

1923 Advertisement for the
Willing Worker Lawn Mower.

Developing leaders in the middle

TWO MINUTES into mowing the grass in our back garden one Easter Saturday the belt broke. The belt drives the blades and the mower is useless without it. I went to B&Q. They had brown belts and yellow belts, but no black belts like the one on my elderly model. I explained my problem to an assistant. He said, '*Take the yellow belt. I think it will work, but slit the packet carefully here and if it doesn't fit return it to me and we will swap it. If I'm not here tell my colleagues in my department what I told you. My name is Dennis*'.

As it happens the belt did fit but Dennis didn't just help me that morning. I was so impressed that I, normally a fickle customer, have since shopped exclusively at the same store spending a couple of hundred pounds over the course of a year. I have also told maybe a dozen friends, now I'm telling you. I'm sure that Dennis didn't pick me out for special treatment. I expect he does the same for others – maybe ten times a week. If everyone in this expanded chain reacts as I did, Dennis is generating an additional £1,152,000 worth of business for B&Q in a 48-week year. If 75% do not react as I did but just 25% do, Dennis is still worth more than fourteen times his annual salary.

Dennis shows what can be achieved when power and responsibility are to be found in the same place and in equal measure. He felt that he had the power to take responsibility. How many situations can we all think of where we have received such an indifferent service that we have decided to take our custom elsewhere as a result of the experience and perhaps tell a dozen friends? The arithmetic also works in reverse.

It is the essence of unconditional leadership that power should not be concentrated only in the hands of those who hold senior positions. There is no point in telling the shop-floor assistant they're a valued member of the team, sharing responsibility for the company's performance, if they don't have the power to exercise an appropriate level of judgement. This is not simply a question of redefining roles. As with so many stories in this collection there are also softer skills in play. I don't know whether Dennis' behaviour reflected company policy, or that of the branch or even of a small team of colleagues, but I do know that he felt confident because he knew that he was trusted. He didn't say, *'don't tell anyone I said so'* (how often have we heard that?). He volunteered his name, actively embracing responsibility. Whoever they were, Dennis' leaders had got the best out of him by making a leader out of him. He was, within a limited ambit, trusted with power and had the confidence to take responsibility. He was leading from the middle.

> ...power should not be concentrated only in the hands of those who hold senior positions

If Dennis' behaviour is so obviously good practice why devote so much space to him? A subsequent foray down the high street that same weekend reveals the answer – assistants were bored, unhelpful, hiding, actively minimising business in shop after shop. Dennis' example may be obvious but it is also relatively rare. Why? I can almost hear the protests of the managers who employ them: *'how can we possibly trust our employees with power or have confidence in them to take responsibility – you've seen what they're like?'*

In part it is chicken and egg. Dennis was lively and pro-active because he was well led. Strip him of power and responsibility and he would be shrinking behind the shelves and shrugging off the customers. It's also about passion – a curiously unfashionable idea but I think it is so important that I devote a whole section to it. Whilst raising money to launch Community Links I took temporary work as a residential social worker in a very large childrens' home. I remember being interviewed for this, my first proper job. The Superintendent explained that many of the children were emotionally damaged and displayed serious behavioural problems. *'You're young'*, he said. *'Might you not take their problems home?' 'I suppose I might,'* I said sheepishly and immediately regretted it. I presumed that I'd blown my chances with this unprofessional response and was very surprised to receive the job offer two days later. When I eventually left the home I asked the Superintendent why I'd been appointed after answering incorrectly. His reply has informed my judgement in appointing staff ever since. *'I'm not interested'*, he said *'in employees who have so little commitment that they don't take the problems home.'*

I am no longer sheepish about passion. I think unconditional leaders communicate and, more important, demonstrate their enthusiasm for the job in hand. They demand the same of those around them. In an environment where everyone feels passionate about what they are doing we don't shrink from power and responsibility, we hunger for it. We all become leaders from the middle even, as Dennis has shown, from the most lowly positions.

Being responsible for a part of the enterprise doesn't mean that we are responsible for everything. At Community Links we experimented in the early years with a collective style of leadership which shared everything equally – decision-making and cleaning. It worked for a small agency but became increasingly untenable as the organisation grew because it denied individuality and de-skilled everyone. We realised that it is possible to develop distinct roles and to distribute power and responsibility selectively whilst maintaining a sense of shared ownership. Unconditional leaders help us to understand that though individually we are laying bricks, or fitting windows, or painting doors, collectively we are building the finest cathedral in the world.

> **In an environment where everyone feels passionate about what they are doing we don't shrink from power and responsibility, we hunger for it**

A sense of ownership in this context is not about a physical asset. It is about the values and the objectives and it is about understanding that we each have a relationship to the whole that is greater than our contribution to the sum of the parts. Does it matter? Did it matter to Dennis? I suspect it did. I imagine he is proud of B&Q, he feels part of something bigger than himself. He may not literally have a share of the assets but he considers himself to be a stakeholder. He rose to the challenge of power and responsibility because he felt confident that he was trusted in an environment where helpfulness and enthusiasm and, yes, passion were encouraged and the sum total was a sense of ownership. He not only belonged to B&Q in the literal contractual sense but also felt that B&Q belonged to him: 'my department'.

I don't deny that it may be easier to generate these feelings in an organisation like Community Links or the children's home where the purpose is so obviously engaging, but that's why I began with Dennis. If it can be achieved on the shop floor, in the local branch of a particularly large retail chain, it can surely be done anywhere.

I often tell colleagues at Community Links that we're not planting mustard and cress, we're growing trees. This is partly a reference to our work where we tackle long-term and deep-rooted problems. Real sustainable solutions will never be quick and easy. It is also, however, a metaphor for the kind of organisation that I want us to create. Charles Handy has shown how family owned businesses are consistently best at planning for the long term. Contrast their priorities with the frequently miserable and sometimes scandalous performance of corporate management teams, where there is no sense of shared ownership and all that it implies. Exploiting short-term shareholder value is their only goal. If we want to lead, as I have wanted to lead, a stable movement capable not only of quick wins but of sustainable developments, we need to ensure that a sense of ownership is shared as surely and as extensively as we share power and responsibility.

> at Community Links... we're not planting mustard and cress, we're growing trees

At Community Links, 80% of our services are delivered by people who first became involved as users, have done training with us and are now working as volunteers or as professionals within the team. This approach builds commitment, loyalty and, ultimately, ownership. It wouldn't work for every organisation but the idea that people want to commit to organisations that have demonstrated a commitment to them is universally applicable.

Take, for example, the mother whose children had made use of Community Links' playschemes and who first talked to staff about the possibility of doing voluntary work. She had been married to an alcoholic and abusive partner. As a result, her confidence and self-esteem were very low. She could not consider applying anywhere for paid work. We suggested a quiet role in the advice team which did not involve direct contact with the public. She began with filing and updating the Information System. After a few months she began taking telephone messages and answering general enquiries about the service.

As her confidence and self-esteem began to rise, she became interested in the advice work going on around her. So when the Advice Manager suggested she join the Community Links training course for advice workers, she agreed. After nine months she achieved an NVQ Level 3 qualification in advice and guidance. She then volunteered as an open door advice worker with Community Links. After six months she successfully applied for a paid post. Over the last three years her confidence and responsibilities have gradually increased. Last year she took part in delivering the Advice work training which she had herself received and this year she was appointed Advice Team Assistant Manager.

> power and responsibility, trust and confidence, ownership and investment – these are all reciprocal relationships

We have undertaken a lot of work in recent years on in-house training programmes, skills audits, personal development plans, all designed not only to increase the capacity of our workforce but also to cement the bond between the individual and the whole and that, in essence, is what this section is all about: power and responsibility, trust and confidence, ownership and investment – these are all reciprocal relationships. As the leader invests more in the team, so the team will produce greater returns for the leadership.

Effective leadership is thus a two-way process. Without responsibility power is dangerous; without power, responsibility is impotent. Without confidence, trust is misplaced; without trust, confidence is foolhardy. Without investment, a sense of ownership will evaporate. Without a sense of ownership, investment will be wasted. When these are in equilibrium everyone – even those in the most inauspicious positions – can lead from the middle and maximise the performance of the entire enterprise.

Community Links' workers and young project participants.

Cultivating Passion

TOUCHED ON PASSION in the last section. I want to explore it a little more carefully here. When I use the word in the context of management or leadership I often feel it generates a certain embarrassment. It seems to be out of step with a modern, thrusting drive for success. On the contrary, I think it's the key to maximising achievement.

Cromwell's dictum, '*every man should know what he fights for and love what he knows*' put knowledge first, because we cannot feel passionate about something we do not understand. After understanding comes feeling. We begin to empathise with the object of the exercise, '*to love what we know*'. Belief – a passionate intellectual commitment – is the result of combining understanding and feeling. Passion is knowledge on fire.

Knowledge is the easy bit. We can state the facts about why we are undertaking a particular mission without creating empathy. Even a manifestly worthwhile objective will not necessarily generate strong feelings unless it is expressed in terms with which we can personally identify. We might read the facts about famine in Africa, but it is the story of the individual family in the fundraising leaflet, the picture of the mother and the child on the TV that produces the emotional response. I often tell potential supporters that they can read the headlines, '*120,000 non-school attenders*', and think, '*I cannot do anything about that, the problem is too big for me*'. Alternatively, they can listen to the volunteers

in our education project when they tell you, '*we did do something for Mustava, we did do something for Lisa*'.

By reducing the big issue to the individual, the personal, it is possible to establish a connection with our own life experience. We can see how we can make a difference to one child. We can then connect the two and believe that we can make a contribution to reducing the problem of non-school attendance.

In the early 1980s Community Links was heavily involved in the Newham Tenants' Tower Block Campaign (NTBTC), which successfully battled for the demolition of the notorious Ronan Point and then went on to campaign for enhanced child-safely measures in high-rise blocks. The local council, burdened by increasing demands on its inadequate resources, resisted the pressure, even after toddler David Cash was killed in an accident falling from a tower block balcony. The Housing Director reached retirement age later that year. NTBTC organised a retirement presentation in the car park on his final day. It was an enormous gold watch made from cardboard, displaying the time and date when, as the inscription explained, '*time stood still for David Cash*'. It was a brutal gesture to a decent man and I can still remember his expression of bewildered horror, which was captured in the evening paper and the regional TV news. Policies, however, were changed within eight weeks.

> **Belief – a passionate intellectual commitment – is the result of combining understanding and feeling**

I have told this story to many audiences over the years and often get the same response, '*Ah, but it is easy to generate passion around an issue like child safety, particularly when it is focused by an appalling tragedy. Under such exceptional circumstances any half-decent leader could galvanise a following and persuade them to do extraordinary things. My issues are routine, my people are ordinary*'.

I always respond with another very different story. Several summers back, my children and I watched a dolphin display. My daughter was entranced and we stayed behind after the other spectators had left. I asked the trainer how she persuaded the dolphin to jump through the hoop several metres above the water. I had never seen such an extraordinary thing. '*We don't start there*', she said, '*we start with the hoop in the water and the food on the other side. The dolphin swims through to reach the treat. Next day we raise the hoop just centimetres and repeat the reward. So the process continues, each day a little higher, until the top of the hoop is out of the water, then the bottom and ultimately the whole thing is well above the surface'.*

Like the dolphins, we all have the potential to do extraordinary things, given the right leadership. This means that we should not start with, metaphorically, the hoop held high and a shouted command. We begin with the ordinary and the reward. Then we stretch, patiently, relentlessly. We maximise performance; ultimately we achieve the extraordinary.

I am reminded of the manager of the Community Links Open Door Advice Service – a responsible, difficult and demanding job. The colleague who fills this role with expertise, good humour and endless patience began her association with CL as a service user. When first invited to become a volunteer she hesitated – 'I don't think I could do that'. But eventually she did. Come September there was a chance to join our NVQ Advice Work Training Course. 'I don't think I could do that' she said. But she could. Two years and one NVQ later a paid job arose. Still 'I don't think…' but still she did. After 3 years in this role the managers position became vacant. This time only the briefest hesitation 'I think I could do that' she said. And she can. Small steps to a big job.

> **we all have the potential to do extraordinary things, given the right leadership**

Cultivating passion is therefore about communicating information (knowing what we fight for), personalising that knowledge (loving what we know), and recognising that for most people in most circumstances this is a learning process. It will not happen over-night. It takes time, unconditional time, to build loyalty, commitment and belief. The process may at times seem long and slow. It is only when we look back and compare past and present performance that we can see how very gradual and incremental progress can eventually lead to extraordinary achievements. Passion – an emotional bond – is not a touchy feely extra. It is a characteristic of the people involved in any successful enterprise. Think about political movements, football teams, community groups you know. Think about those that succeed and those that fail. Passion is the mojo.

Don't just do
something...
dream!

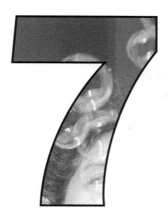

Valuing the Individual

I HAVE SUGGESTED THAT an effective leader will establish a culture where trust and confidence will flourish, where a sense of ownership characterises the relationship between the individual and the whole, and where an emotional bond is as important as any formal contract. Such relationships begin with a process of 'small learning', cherishing the tiny but cumulative steps which culminate in the dolphin clearing the hoop ten metres from the water. Small learning requires the provision of continuous opportunities to train and develop. This has two effects, First, it gives us the skills to do a new or better job. Second, it gives us confidence and belief in our own capacity for making a useful contribution.

I can never think about training without remembering an article in our internal bulletin. The writer was an advice service volunteer hoping to return to work after a very difficult period in her life. She completed our NVQ course in advice and guidance and she recalled an image from a children's book of the little train chugging up the hill... (I *think* I can, I *think* I can, I *think* I can), then reaching the top and swooping down the other side (I *know* I can, I *know* I can, I *know* I can). That is exactly how training should make everybody feel, and why no

THE LITTLE ENGINE THAT COULD

successful enterprise should ever be so short of time or money that learning cannot be given the priority it deserves.

Without the relevant skills or knowledge it is impossible to believe in our own ability but these prerequisites alone are not enough to generate self-belief. We all need encouragement, positive affirmation and we need good rôle models; not just people who show us how it is done, but more importantly, inspire us to do it for ourselves.

The football manager Ron Atkinson's injured striker was receiving attention from the trainer. *'He is concussed,'* the trainer shouted across to his manager. *'Take him off. He does not know his own name'.* *'He is concussed,'* replied Atkinson. *'Leave him on. Tell him he is Pele'.*

My seven-year-old son plays football with children who think that they are David Beckham, Michael Owen or Joey Cole. They are not, and most of them never will, be but that is not the point. Simply pretending to be somebody else does not make us that person, but by identifying with the best we are setting our sights as high as we can. We may fall short, but we are stretching ourselves, striving, aspiring and it is through this endeavour that we continually improve. Leaders create the environment where it is considered either cocky, pretentious or plain silly to dream of exceptional performance, or where it is commonplace to be, in the words of our statement *'driven by dreams, judged on delivery'.*

I once had a science teacher who would regularly bellow: *'Don't just SIT there dreaming. Do SOMETHING!'* There are times in the hurly-burly of modern life when I think it would be helpful if a neon sign flashed in our brains carrying the same words, but in a different order: *'Don't just do something. DREAM!'*

Making the time and space to do this for ourselves can be difficult. Helping others to create the same opportunity is even more challenging, but the unconditional leader will have the confidence and the common sense to appreciate the long-term benefits. A recent Community Links' publication – *Holding up the Sky* – is a powerful and thought-provoking story of a community development project in a South African village told from the perspective of an experienced development worker. Author Trish Bartley drew her title from an African proverb: *'If everyone helps to hold up the sky, then one person does not become tired*'. Dreaming the big dreams is not the responsibility of one person. It is a job for us all.

Feeling secure with this approach requires not only the small practical learning to which I have referred but also the personal example of a relationship. Mentoring is a fashionable word, which has come to mean many things in recent years. I use it here to distinguish between the conventional functions of line-management – primarily concerned with what we do – and the complementary but different approach that is needed to develop how we do it. Though ultimately the two are inseparable, the mentoring approach, as I have described it, focuses primarily on the process and not the product. We tend to think of the mentor and the manager as different people and this often works well. However, I think a strong leader needs to be capable of playing both parts. The conventional command and control structure prizes the tough manager above all else. The unconditional leader places the greater emphasis on enabling team members to solve their own problems, not by providing ready-made solutions but by helping them to identify the answers within themselves. Mentees should feel supported in a variety of ways which would not normally characterise a traditional management relationship.

- ■ **A CONFIDENTIAL LISTENER** Mentors listen hard but say little in the relationship and nothing outside it.

- ■ **A THREE-SIDED MIRROR** Mentors reflect the problem which the Mentee projects, but which can only be seen in its entirety with the help of others. They reflect it back from new angles.

- ■ **A HOLY FOOL** Mentors are at least one step removed from the day-to-day problem. Their naïve questions will reveal biased judgements, prejudices and irrational feelings.

- ■ **A HIGHLIGHTER** Mentors identify the most significant aspect of a problem, not the noisiest or the most demanding.

- ■ **AN ADVISOR** Mentors offer the wisdom of an alternative experience. They say, 'have you thought', not, 'I think you should'.

- ■ **A GUIDE** Mentors listen and reflect back. They ask searching questions, highlight significant issues and contribute their experience. The path emerges and the Mentor and the Mentee identify it together. Both have learnt but have not been taught.

An important organisational point emerges here. Don't do anything I have suggested if you want all your people to be identical. I recently watched a TV documentary about a chain of estate agents. The point wasn't made in the film but I noticed that all the sales people were white, 20- to 30-year-old males, tackling the job from very similar perspectives. Commanding and controlling them was not particularly difficult for their leader, who was perhaps 35, but otherwise a clone, but I wondered if the team would not have been more successful if it had included a wider range of life experiences. They would have approached the job from different angles and offered customers a choice. I appreciate that they would also have been much harder to lead, but the development of individual contributions would have substantially enhanced the collective offering.

> **Unconditional listening time is the greatest gift which we can give to another person**

Valuing the individual will accentuate the positive differences. Each worker will be developing their own unique contribution. They won't fit so easily into a tidy structure. Organising a team in this context requires us to audit qualities as well as functions, but we will then have a team of many dimensions and diverse qualities, growing and changing all the time. A truly living organisation and as Lord Shepperd, then Chairman of Grand Metropolitan, once told me, 'only cemeteries have people in tidy rows'.

All this demands time to *listen*. If there is a single lesson which I draw from our experience, it is the importance of this point. In the early days of Community Links I dominated the discussions at the trustees' meeting. It became a standing joke that I talked for most of the time. I thought this showed strong leadership. I was on top of all the issues. Gradually I became disillusioned with the meetings. I would prepare carefully for them, work hard on my own contribution but get nothing back. Others seldom influenced or informed the decisions that I had already made. I began to wonder if we had got the wrong trustees until slowly I started to see that it was I who had got it wrong.

Unconditional listening time is the greatest gift which we can give to another person. It says, and it means, I value you and believe in you. Also, that I can learn from you and that I need you. Motivation, stimulation, inspiration flow both ways. I try very hard now never to speak first in meetings in which I might be considered to be the leader and I strictly limit my contributions to the discussion.

Sadly, however, the scarcity of time is often paraded as a measure of importance – '*I can give you ten minutes*' – and the inability to listen as an indicator of authority. How shallow and short-sighted. We achieve so little on our own. Leaders who are not informing their own judgements with the experience of others, not working night and day to maximise those contributions, are simply ignoring their most accessible asset. No matter how talented or driven the leader, individual capacity is finite. Listening is the multiplier. Leaders who encourage contributions from the widest range of participants without reference to status or structure are thus the most likely to achieve extraordinary results. We have two ears and one mouth. Intelligent leaders use them in that order.

If listening is the most obvious way of both demonstrating and acting on your belief in others, it is not the only way. Never underestimate the value of the small but significant gesture. I remember a low period when I was working alone and from home, shaping my ideas for Community Links. Progress was slow. I would watch the postman walking down the street like it was my birthday and I was eight years old. Often he walked straight past. One day he delivered a small package. Inside were 50 postage stamps, no letter nor any trace of identity. The gesture was repeated several times over the first difficult year. I had no idea who sent them, but they lifted my spirits and urged me forward. Their value was incalculable.

I wrote to the directors of the big national charities – many are still around. Most never answered. Some replied but were too busy to see me. Several did make the time and then used it to criticise our ideas and undermine my confidence! I was young, probably naïve, but well-intentioned and deeply dispirited. Then Alec Dickson rang. He was the founder of CSV and VSO – two of the UK's biggest voluntary agencies. He made the time to see me, once, then again and intermittently for the rest of his life. He rang on Christmas Eve at the end of the first slow year to wish Community Links, with characteristic brevity, a 'successful New Year'. I asked him at our second meeting if I should give up, perhaps try again when I was older as so many had advised. 'Do you still believe that your ideas are worthwhile?', he asked. 'I do,' I said. 'Then you go on.' It was not advice, it was an order.

Alec was an unconditional leader. He taught me many things, some helped immediately. One, perhaps the most important, I have grown to appreciate; on our own, our achievements are limited no matter what position we may attain. It is through encouraging, supporting and inspiring others that our dreams take flight and that we break free from the constraints of personal capacity. Never stop listening. Never stop sharing your vision and the visions of others.

Sometimes, despite meticulous
planning, things don't turn out
the way we hoped.

John Loengard/Time & Life Pictures/Getty Images

Appreciating failure

L ISTENING IMPLIES a willingness to embrace change. Change entails a measure of risk. Over my working life I think the voluntary sector in which I operate has become more and more risk-averse. I do not have the experience to make a judgement about other sectors, although I suspect that the same may be true elsewhere, and that these trends reflect a society-wide demand for endeavouring to eliminate risk wherever we might find it. At Community Links, for instance, our under-fives' provision over the years has been substantially affected by legislation which now lays down minimum standards for everything from child to leader ratios, through to the nature of the guards on the radiators.

Soaring insurance premiums indicate what, as a society, we expect in redress from those who fail us. It is hard to argue with any changes which make the world a safer place or a better place, but I think this has all had a cumulative effect on the national psyche. There is now a danger of regarding risk – any risk – as a bad thing, without recognising that very little progress can be achieved without it. We need to recognise that there are different kinds of risk and different kinds of failures.

Attempting to run an under-fives' project in premises which are unsuitable for the purpose and without observing the safety regulations is an unacceptable risk. If there were then an accident and the playgroup closed down we would be guilty of a 'bad failure' resulting from our own incompetence and negligence.

Compare this with an attempt to run, say, a different kind of playgroup, focusing on a particularly hard-to-reach group. We might experiment with different kinds of publicity, the provision of transport to and from the group, offers and inducements for parents and children, but still the playgroup might fail to attract sufficient numbers and eventually close down. In my book, this would have been, an acceptable risk. A genuine attempt to develop a new service to meet a new need explored in a variety of creative and innovative ways. In the end the attempt was unsuccessful, but not because we were negligent or incompetent. We can expect to develop our understanding from this experience, with lessons which could not have been learned any other way. This is a 'good failure'.

> '...good failures...will be out-numbered by the successes, but a complete absence of failure is the hallmark of timid and fearful leadership'

Well-led organisations are those whose CV's are sprinkled with good failures. They will be outnumbered of course by the successes, but a complete absence of failure is the hallmark of timid and fearful leadership.

Several years ago a friend in government was seconded from the Treasury to spend a year in a venture capital company. He would be selecting companies for investment and was told, as part of his induction, to plan for four failures out of 10. If he achieved less than that (say, if 8, 9, or even 10 of his investments were successful), he would be investing at the wrong point in the risk curve. His choices would have been the 'safe bets', companies that could have borrowed from a high street bank.

Like all 'safe bets' they would have been unlikely to fail, but equally will never yield a big return. My friend contrasted this advice with his experience in the Treasury. If he had applied the same approach on his return to Whitehall he would have been 'consigned to a basement office in the Ministry of Agriculture' for the rest of his career.

Every leader has to find the point on the risk curve that is appropriate for their work and is comfortable for them, but I take the view that progress is dependant upon innovation, that innovation is rarely risk-free and that good failures are, in amongst the successes, one of the hallmarks of unconditional leadership.

When I was first asked to write this collection I was overcome with self-doubt. I found myself thinking of all the things I have done wrong in my career, all the aspects of our work at the moment that could be better. Then I realised that that, in a sense, is the point of unconditional leadership. We are not striving for a perfect state, an end point where nothing could be improved. If we ever feel that we have reached that stage we have either lost touch with reality or stopped pushing forward the objectives to the point where the whole exercise has ground to a halt. Either way, we have given up any claim to leadership.

Linus Pauling is a man who knew more than most about leadership, risk and innovation. He won Nobel Prizes in two different disciplines and once said *'the way to have a good idea is to have lots of ideas'*. Jimmy Greaves made a similar point on a more prosaic subject. When asked for the secret behind his high-scoring career he replied *'I took a lot of shots'*. The lesson is the same whatever the field of endeavour: no progress without risk, no risk without failure.

I was recently asked to make a presentation to an audience of business leaders on *'Community Links: the success factors'*, I was irritated by the complacency of the brief and suggested that the 'failure factors' might be more useful. I read a couple of paragraphs from one of our earliest Annual Reports:

> *'In the summer of 1981 we set up and ran an adventure playground on a piece of vacant land on the Folkestone Road Estate. It was a summer of great highs and great lows. The management in the neighbouring factory were hostile. The site was strewn with rubble and many hours of very heavy work went into preparing for the scheme. We bought two mobile builder's huts at considerable expense because we needed to store equipment somewhere secure and water proof. We invested in materials and fencing and paid seasonal staff to ensure that the playground was properly supervised in every daylight hour. It was an enormous success. Children made the playground into a second home, building camps and dens and each one having a space to develop something for themselves.*

> *'By the end of the summer we knew that the experiment had been such a success that we had to make it permanent, despite continuing*

opposition from the factory. We invested in making the huts more secure for the long winter nights and ordered security fencing before we knew how we would pay for it.

'One Sunday night in late September the fire brigade telephoned. By the time we got to the playground it was engulfed in flames, which had already spread to the roof of the factory. Three fire engines were fighting a losing battle. Eventually the bulk of the factory was saved although very badly damaged. The playground was completely destroyed and still smoking when the contactors arrived next morning to put up the high security fencing. We sent them away but still had to find £900 for their materials before we began the much more serious argument about liability for the factory. For a while it looked like Community Links had burned to death that Sunday night. Eventually the insurance company covered the major liability but it was the end of the playground. It seemed that the hut had been visited by a couple of boys to sniff glue. They had brought candles to see what they were doing, one got knocked over.'

Just re-reading these lines gives me a hollow feeling in the pit of my stomach, but that dreadful September night was as important to the subsequent development of Community Links as any of the, thankfully, more numerous successes. Wellington believed that armies could best be judged on *'how they take a pounding'*. Strong leaders would never knowingly head for disaster but nor should they shrink from a challenge. The early success of the playground had shown us that there was a need for children's facilities which were outside the mainstream provision and that, with an entirely different approach we could involve the 'hard to reach'. We had learned a huge amount in three short months. The lessons were to inform the development of the Youth Work Programme in which we now work with 3,000 children every week. The experience toughened the team, hardened its resolve and strengthened its commitment. The solicitor who faced the factory managers and the insurance company is still the chair of our trustees until just last year; the inventor and the manager of the playground is now a Senior Adviser. It did not feel much like it at the time but the playground was a good failure.

Good failures are a reasonable, if ultimately unsuccessful response to evidence of need and are, crucially, rooted in the values of the organisation. I started this section with a reference to the importance of *'embracing change'*, but in the section on values I specifically excluded the value-base from this continuous dynamic progression. Values are, I emphasised, *'the abiding moral base, constant and enduring'*. But moral certainty should not restrict ambition or the taking of risk. It should liberate, stimulate and challenge for, as Billy Bragg has sung, *'Virtue never tested is no virtue at all'*.

The development of the Canning Town Public Hall was another milestone for the Community Links' management. There are two stories I want to tell about that. Actually it is the same story, but I want to tell it twice:

① There once was a charity in East London, which, after ten years of successful development had out-grown its home and was looking for opportunities to move. The Canning Town Public Hall, once a fine Town Hall, was now empty and rapidly becoming run-down and derelict. The organisation suggested to the local council that it would take on the hall and bring it back into community use at no cost to the Council, if the authority would transfer the asset. An agreement was reached. The organisation would deliver on its offer within two years and receive the building. If it failed, the building would revert back to the council with anything that the organisation had put into it. Almost one million pounds worth of goods, services and materials in kind were then contributed by 127 companies. A further £500,000 was raised in cash, and a fully renovated and modernised and equipped building was duly opened two years later. It now serves around 4,000 people every week.

② *Alternatively*… There once was a charity in East London, which had been heavily dependent on grant-aid from the Greater London Council. When the GLC was disbanded some of the grants were picked up by other bodies, but some were lost forever. The organisation, unwilling to contemplate redundancy or the termination of essential services, reduced salaries equally across the board and stopped paying the Inland Revenue whilst frantically fund-raising. Managers knew that this policy was sustainable as long as the debt did not exceed the value of the property they owned. Nine months on, the debt was still rising and now into six figures, but an exciting plan had been developed to relocate into the Canning Town Public Hall. It was a brave vision which inspired supporters but it required a complex deal with the local authority and one which was very far from agreed when the bombshell hit.

Suddenly somebody remembered that the property was valued at the height of the Docklands property boom but the market had since plummeted. A hasty revaluation revealed a dreadful gap in the arithmetic. The building was sold urgently in auction before anything was agreed on the new premises. The purchasers and the Inland Revenue were stalled and delayed until agreement on the Hall was sealed in the nick of time. The organisation moved immediately into the unlit, unheated derelict building in order to 'to demonstrate our commitment to unleashing the potential of this exciting place'. It is also true that they had nowhere else to go. Receipts from the old building cleared half of the tax debt and allowed a two-year repayment schedule to be agreed. New partners were excited and inspired by the new vision and within two years the debts were cleared, the renovated public hall was re-opened and now serves around 4,000 people every week.

The two stories begin and end identically and neither is untrue. It is all a matter of presentation. I don't think good leaders lie, but I do think they are responsible not only for finding the solutions but also for finding the most positive way of expressing the challenge. Henry Ford said, *'believe you can or believe you can't, either way you will be right'*. In a complex world few challenges are without their ups and downs. Communicating the positive whilst tackling the negative does not guarantee success but it maximises the chances. It is like a driver skidding on ice; you can put your foot on the brakes and maybe slow down a little before you slide into the wall, or you can put your foot on the accelerator and attempt to drive out of the skid. You might still smack into the wall. Alternatively you may pull away far faster than before.

> **Unconditional leadership is leadership which is uninhibited by the fear of failure**

Was the John Stonehouse experience which I recounted in the second chapter a failure or a success? Some of our critics condemned our association with a convicted fraudster and suggested that our own reputation would be irrevocably damaged. Others admired the chutzpah, envied the media coverage and appreciated the practical benefits. At the time, of course, I was firmly in the latter camp. Now I recognise that the adventure had its advantages and disadvantages, but given the same circumstances again I'd focus on the positive and take the risk every time.

I share these experiences because I am on a mission to bring failure out of the closet. Unconditional leadership is leadership which is uninhibited by the fear of failure. It is not blind to risk; on the contrary it has a discerning eye for distinguishing between bad failure which it avoids, and good failure which it celebrates. It accentuates the positive, learns from the negative, and understands that innovation and ultimately growth can only be sustained through a combination of the two.

Many years ago I came across a poem by Christopher Logue. It seemed to say everything I wanted to say about the Community Links approach to risk and, more widely, about the kind of organisation that I wanted us to be. I wrote to the publishers asking if I could include it in our Annual Report. Several weeks elapsed and I forgot the request. Then, out of the blue, Christopher rang. We talked for a long time about Community Links and the poem. He said I could use it as I thought best. I'd like to use it here.

Come to the edge.
We might fall.
Come to the edge.
It's too high.
Come to the edge!
And they came and they pushed.
And they flew.

Christopher Logue

During the Victorian era some of the most profound changes in technology and society were initiated, not least the origination of mass communication by affordable mail services.

Pacing the change

'Change? Why do we need change?
Things are quite bad enough as they are.'

Queen Victoria

I N ONE OF MY FIRST PLACEMENTS as a relief worker in a childrens' home, I found myself working under a particularly strict regime. The twelve children, all under ten, were not allowed to speak during meal times. Staff, who ate separately, patrolled in silence. I and another new young worker were disturbed by this approach. We thought meal times were for sharing, that we should eat with the children, encourage them to talk. Older staff were dismissive of the idea. It would, they said, end in tears, but we persevered. Eventually the two of us were on duty together with no other staff. We sat down to eat with the children and struck up a conversation. At first no-one responded, but gradually the noise level rose …and rose… children were shouting from one table to another. Then a chip went over my head, followed by more. Someone was under the table, someone was crying. It was already ending in tears and we hadn't begun the rice pudding.

I was deeply dispirited by this failure. The children had let me down badly. The older staff were right. The experience appeared to prove that everything that I believed about good residential social work was naïve and impractical.

I didn't resolve the dilemma that summer, but I have often reflected on it when working with new staff colleagues who have been accustomed to a very different working environment. We often, for instance, work with secondees from government who spend maybe 6 or 9 months with us. Almost all these career civil servants have been diligent and effective and have opened up new possibilities for the development of our work, but almost all have also struggled, in the early weeks, with a working environment that encourages more responsibility and self-discipline than they have exercised in the past, expects more innovation and demands greater flexibility. None of them have yet thrown a fish-finger at me but I can see the parallels.

Those who are accustomed to obeying instructions know how to behave within a regimented regime. Take away those rules and it is difficult then, at least at first, to find the right way of behaving. The children who had previously understood talking to be a cardinal offence were now being encouraged to converse. If conversation was now allowed, why not shouting, food throwing, table walking? We had taken away the clear and rigid set of parameters, assuming that this would allow 'normal behaviour' to flourish, but for those who had never been trained in our definition of 'normality' there were now no reference points. There was nothing wrong with our objective but we were expecting far too much, far too soon from people whose life experience had been different from our own.

> **we were expecting far too much, far too soon from people whose life experience had been different from our own**

Change can be enforced overnight, but will rarely carry hearts and minds. Alternatively, it can be *embraced*, but this is a gradual process, recognising that everybody's life experience is different and that what might be obvious to us is an entirely new idea to somebody else. This shouldn't lessen our commitment to change – I wish now that I had persevered at the childrens' home – but it should inform the process. *'Social change won't come overnight,'* said Martin Luther King. *'But we must always work as though it were a possibility in the morning'*. The pace is critical. Too slow and we lose commitment, too fast and we lose our following.

When Charles Darwin observed that it was neither the strongest nor the most intelligent species that survived, but the one that was most responsive to change, he could have been writing about the unconditional leader – a leader who is not inhibited by history or convention but is constantly willing to experiment with the new. This involves the recognition that the process will rarely be straightforward or tidy. Whilst it may not always be necessary to go through the food throwing, metaphorically or otherwise, change invariably unsettles. I was recently talking to a colleague who was unhappy about changes in her job. *'But all these changes,'* I said, *'are addressing problems which you have been grumbling about'*. *'Ahhh, yes,'* she replied, *'but I enjoy grumbling'*.

Change moves us from our comfort zone. That can be threatening, but is also, in part, the point of the exercise. Successful leadership is characterised neither by relentless stagnation, nor by the stop-start cycle of change which is often mistaken for dynamic leadership. In a moment of rare candour Donald Rumsfeld once observed that American governments do two things well – nothing and over-reaction. The same could be said of many organisations – not just large ones. *'Governing a great country,'* said Lau Tsu, *'is like cooking a small fish. Don't over-do it'*. When you are next tempted to make sweeping and dramatic change think small fry. Consistently strong leadership isn't primarily about doing extraordinary things occasionally, but doing ordinary things better and better, day-by-day.

> **Change moves us from our comfort zone. That can be threatening, but is also, in part, the point of the exercise**

Effective leaders will help with the shifts from the comfort zone by explaining the change carefully and at a very early stage with, wherever possible, the opportunity to entertain alternative ideas. Transparency is especially important. I think there have been many times when I haven't meant to be secretive; it just didn't occur to me to make the information available when I should have done. Such leadership nourishes conspiracy theories and unsettles everybody. I sometimes think it might be a good idea to circulate a transcript from the most private meetings, on the basis that no-one reads minutes but gossip spreads like wildfire around discussions known to be confidential. Perhaps that's going too far, but I think transparency – wherever possible – limits uncertainty, reduces fear and maximises participation in the process and ownership of the outcome.

Nowhere is this more important than in the process of succession-planning for key posts. I've read about leaders who begin the process on the day of their appointment. I can't claim such powers of forethought, but I do think that unconditional leaders discourage the kind of 'mighty oak' approach which makes succession very difficult. The oak, magnificent in many ways, is so dominant that acorns falling from the tree can never develop properly in its shadow. The ones which grow into oak trees are those which are moved elsewhere by birds or squirrels.

> *...never changing is not an option. Changing steadily and constantly is demanding but essential*

By taking some of the steps outlined elsewhere in this collection, we are ensuring that the organisation offers fertile territory for the development of the next generation. Thus change within that territory does not need to be imposed from outside, but can be developing steadily and constantly. Equally, the products of our development process do not need to go elsewhere to find fulfilment of their own potential.

Holding Up The Sky

Love, Power and Learning
in the Development of a Community

TRISH BARTLEY

communitylinks

Whether we are considering people or entire organisations the principles are the same; never changing is not an option. Changing steadily and constantly is demanding but essential.

Holding up the Sky concluded with a Rumi poem which uses language that might seem more appropriate in a South African village than in modern Europe. Sometimes an entirely new perspective can help us understand a simple truth.

'The breeze at dawn has secrets to tell you.
Don't go back to sleep.
You must ask for what you really want.
Don't go back to sleep.
People are going back and forth across the doorsill
Where the two worlds touch.
The door is round and open.
Don't go back to sleep'.

It is difficult sometimes to see a positive way out of a complex problem!

Maximising Achievement, and what to do when it all goes wrong

P
ERHAPS I SHOULD have begun with a warning. Instead I will end with it. Unconditional leadership is not a soft touch. It is about being open to ideas and also to criticism, about encouraging others to develop, to take risks and to fail, about dialogue and argument, diversity and difference, about training and supporting people to be strong and confident, passionate and rebellious, challenging and provocative. Perhaps, if we don't encounter difficulties from time to time, we are not, to borrow a phrase from another section in this collection, *'investing at the right point in the risk curve'*.

Because I get it wrong, again and again, I want to conclude with some nuggets of advice. They're not exactly golden rules – other ideas in this collection are equally important – but they have all helped me to either manage difficult situations or, better still, to avoid them next time. When I planned this collection I thought of ten tips. That seemed like a neat number. By the time I had finished writing I had thought of eleven. That seems like a good place to start...

① **NEVER STOP LEARNING**   If we do exactly the same thing day after day we might expect to eventually be perfect or at least to make a habit of our imperfections. 'Practice makes permanent', says my friend's music teacher. It is no substitute for continuous learning but it is the easy option. If we keep challenging ourselves with new targets, new approaches seeking to maximise our capacity, we must expect to fail. There is no such thing as an infallible leader, only one who lacks the vision to see, the intelligence to understand or the confidence to acknowledge that we all have more to learn. Ask for help. It may make us vulnerable but it also makes us strong. *'Live like you expect to die tomorrow,'* said Mahatma Gandhi, *'but learn like you expect to live forever'.*

② **SLEEP ON IT**   There is a fine line between decisive leadership and hot-headed impetuosity. Some decisions must be taken immediately – but not all. Learn to distinguish between those which require an instant judgement and those which would benefit from considered reflection. Difficult personnel issues for instance, letters you find particularly hard to write, conflict resolution in complex discussions. Make a decision but don't publicise it, write the letter but don't post it, determine your strategy but don't begin to implement it. Look at it again in the morning. Then commit to action.

③ **TALK**   One-to-one, face-to-face wherever possible. Don't email, text or leave an answerphone message. Difficult situations are resolved by leaders who are brave and open, who are not afraid to be seen to be human and vulnerable and whose opinions and decisions are honest and heartfelt. We may not always agree with the conclusion but we can respect the person and the process.

Two years ago I talked with the Chief Executive of a major company about an ambitious collaboration. It was the beginning of what was to become *We Are What We Do*. We had several meetings over 18 months, shaping the ideas together, and we eventually presented them to his board. I was impressed by his vision, his enthusiasm for new ideas and his leadership. Six weeks later I received his letter. The company had rejected our proposal. I was experienced enough to cope with rejection but I was surprised and disappointed by the style of the Chief Executive's communication. It contrasted sharply with our many warm and exciting conversations when the auguries were promising. He was diminished in my eyes as a man and as a leader.

We feel this issue is sufficiently important to include the following paragraph in an otherwise strictly functional section on emailing in our staff handbook: *'remember, sending an email is sometimes far easier than speaking to someone face to face or even talking on the phone, especially if you have something difficult to say. Once an email has been sent it cannot be retrieved! Don't email in anger. If you have something difficult to say, try to speak to the person face to face where possible or speak to them by phone where this is not practical'.*

④ **BUY A FOUNTAIN PEN** Words are powerful. We have the potential to hurt and to heal, to inform and to inspire with the right words chosen carefully, expressed personally. I have never wanted to be a politician and have had no hesitation in resisting the very occasional invitations to consider the possibility. Two lines from Hugo Young made me almost change my mind. *'Politics'*, he lamented, *'is no longer attracting risk-takers and people of bold category-shifting vision; people who can live at the edge of the possible, ruthless as well as decent people, adventurous as well as honest. People with the brains to be inventive and the guts to be unpopular…'* A simple idea, expressed with vigour, colour and power.

Words can conjure up an image and move us to action or convey exactly the same meaning, but leave us feeling flat and apathetic. On the US Presidential campaign trail in 1988, Michael Dukakis spoke about *'a more decent, compassionate society'*. George Bush Senior's speech writers spun the line, *'a kinder, gentler America'*. Both speeches were poorly delivered but the Bush script, contrary to the substance of his policy, was inspirational, humane and warm. The Dukakis construction was, in comparison, formal, cold, detached.

In our statement of purpose we could have said, *'to generate creative new strategies which are monitored and assessed on an on-going basis'*. We did say, *'to be driven by dreams, judged on delivery'*. We need different words for different purposes. A speech that seeks to inspire should not use the same language as a manual that endeavours to instruct. Previous generations took more care with words than we do today. I'd like to revive the art, because it works. For any aspiring leader the fountain pen is a luxury, but careful use of language is not. Take the time to exploit its potential.

⑤ **MAKE YOUR OWN LUCK** Luck – good and bad – plays a part in the most well-ordered lives. I've read about 'lucky leaders' and there certainly is a lot of evidence to suggest that a number of key figures over the years have just happened to be in the right place at the right time. Scratch beneath the surface, however, and the story is rarely so simple.

Abraham Zapruder was a keen amateur photographer; he rarely went anywhere without a camera. He purchased a top-of-the-range 8mm home-movie camera with a zoom lens to record his grandchildren growing up. On November 22, 1963 he decided not to bring his new camera to work because the morning had been overcast and rainy. But later, the sun broke out and he made a trip back home to fetch the camera. By lunchtime he was in the crowd in Dallas as President Kennedy's motorcade turned into Dealey Plaza. Almost 100 amateur and professional photographers captured images at the  scene as the open-top car drove past the Book Depository. But for Abraham Zapruder his timing, his high-quality camera and a photographer's eye for position made his 26 seconds of film the world's most famous home movie. Good luck is where preparation meets opportunity.

I think we have to realise that leadership, like life itself, is a percentage business. Sometimes you get things right and sometimes you get them wrong. If you keep trying you are more likely to get more things right than if you curl up and die at the first sniff of failure or misfortune. Way back in the early 80s we managed to buy our second centre through a unique mortgage agreement connected to a direct payroll-giving scheme. More than one hundred people were sharing the repayments. It was an unusual arrangement and I remember being told, on several occasions, that we were 'lucky' to find a bank that would agree to it. If it had been the first bank that we had approached I would have agreed. If it had been the fifth or sixth we might have said that we deserved to get lucky. As our proposal to the Williams and Glynn Bank in Cavendish Square was actually our thirteenth attempt to find a partner, I think it's fair to say that we made our own luck.

Don't let a run of bad luck undermine your self-confidence. Remember that the tide turns at low water as well as high.

(6) **VISUALISE THE POSITIVE** Staying positive during the difficult periods is very hard. It's easy to be a positive, buoyant leader in the good times. Ironically, it is even more important in the bad, when we

need leaders to encourage, support and inspire. Leaders who remind us of principles. Leaders in whom we can believe.

I remember some years ago preparing a funding pitch to the Home Office. We were seeking the renewal of grant aid for a project which had not gone to plan. It was a mixture of good failures and bad failures. One of the staff appointments in the small team had been a mistake, we'd met considerable opposition from entrenched interests and we had promised too much in the first place. I was sharing my despondency with an old friend the night before the meeting and she told me that I might as well stay in bed the next morning if I intended to approach the meeting in the same frame of mind. No-one would want to back a project that was led by anybody who couldn't explain the problems confidently and honestly and still exude a 'can do' enthusiasm for the future. She told me to forget the arguments that would be raised at the meeting; I had already done all the preparation that I could on the issues. Instead I should visualise a situation in which I had performed well. It might be at work or at home, recent or well back into my childhood. I had to think about any time when I felt good about myself. I had to recreate that moment in my head. I was sceptical but also desperate, so I gave it a try. It helped me enormously. I kept my head up, I smiled and spoke confidently. The tone and style of my performance was positive and reassuring and the funding was renewed.

It is a simple trick and I have often repeated it before doing anything I might otherwise find difficult. I once appeared on *Newsnight* on BBC2, to talk about changes in the welfare benefits system. Moments before transmission the sound engineer adjusted my microphone. I must have seemed preoccupied because he apologised for interrupting my train of thought saying, '*Don't worry. Paxman's really not as bad as he seems*'. I just smiled, because it would have seemed insufferably cocky for one as inexperienced as me to say, 'I wasn't. I was thinking about my daughter's birthday party'.

⑦ **CHANGE THE ANGLE**
If you are reading this page the usual way you might see a fence. Adjust the angle of the page and you are looking  at a ladder. In times of difficulty it is especially easy to become entrenched in our thinking, to narrow down our perspective.

Suppose there's a personality clash between two key members of the team. We've tried negotiating on the principles of the relationship but it doesn't seem to be about principles. We've tried banging heads together but that just gave everyone a headache. Where now? It's tempting to bore down into even more detail about who said what last Tuesday evening. Suppose instead we talk about expanding the team, introducing new personalities and responsibilities, taking the opportunity of wider change to alter rôles and create space and distance. New responsibilities might necessitate some training, opening up fresh horizons and maybe a break in other routines – a different desk perhaps – and also a long-term plan for further development – something to look forward to. None of this addresses the question of who said what on Tuesday, but it shifts perspective – it no longer seems so important.

We can move on to new territory together without backing down or losing face. The changes are not cosmetic or a con, on the contrary they are real and practical, but they haven't directly addressed the presenting problem in its original narrow frame. We have changed the perspective. We have exploited the Chinese meaning of the word crisis. They use two ideograms to convey the word. One means threat and the other opportunity. Crisis, in the Chinese language is, as in life itself, the relationship between the two.

⑧ **DON'T PERSONALISE**   For years I hated our bank manager. Not that I knew him, of course, but it was his signature on the 'courtesy' letters 'reminding' me that we had exceeded our overdraft limit. It is easy to personalise a problem, but not helpful. At best we shift blame without developing a solution. At worst we create enemies out of people who might otherwise be useful.

Every enterprise can be improved. All of us can do better. Arguing for what might be achieved in the future does not necessarily require us to dismiss or condemn all that has been achieved in the past. My role at Community Links changed four years ago. I am no longer Chief Executive but I still participate in planning for the future. I am excited by innovation and determined to support dynamic, fresh ideas but I am also dispirited when that vision is presented as the solution to a problem. We must all be capable of justifying improvement without necessarily criticising implicitly or explicitly the ways of the past. I used the term 'feminised' to describe this consensual, collaborative approach in the second chapter. I am not sure about the jargon but it seems like common sense to me. It is certainly an important characteristic of inclusive unconditional leadership. We can't build support and establish alliances if we alienate others unnecessarily.

When I shared a draft of this section with a colleague he pointed out that my personal interpretation of the new ideas presented as personal criticism was just that – a personal interpretation – and different from his own. I thought he was right and I deleted the paragraph. On further reflection I've put it back in, not because I now think he was wrong but because he helped me understand that I was inadvertently making another important point – don't personalise and don't always assume that criticism is intended to be personal. When I take my own advice, ask for help (① *above*) and sleep on it (② *above*) I realise that it rarely is.

Creative brainstorms often establish the ground rule that no idea should be criticised. Participants can build on the contribution of the last speaker, or they can ignore it and take the discussion in a different direction, but negativity is not an option. It isn't always possible to adopt the same approach in strategic planning but I believe that life is, for most of us, essentially a prolonged exercise in research and development. I therefore think it is always helpful to speak about doing things better rather than putting things right, to think about next steps rather than problems, to view the planning process as a continual development rather than a response to the weaknesses and inadequacies of the past and, especially when some critique is unavoidable, to consider how it will be interpreted and by whom.

I can think of a number of community leaders that I have seen from afar and some that I have worked with who are deeply committed and brilliant in their own right, but who have been thoughtless or careless on this important point and who have found themselves unnecessarily isolated. There is nothing soft and sentimental about this. It is entirely about the prudent and pragmatic management of scarce resources.

⑨ **BE UNREASONABLE** George Bernard Shaw wrote that, '*Reasonable men attempt to adapt themselves to the world. Unreasonable men attempt to adapt the world to them. Progress is in the hands of unreasonable men*'.

Warren Bennis, founder of the Leadership Institute at the University of Southern California, says that '*leadership*

is the wise use of power. Power is translating intention into reality and sustaining it'. In the end this will sometimes require us to disagree, to stick to a course of action when others are arguing for an alternative, to be unreasonable. This will be difficult but no challenge worth meeting will ever be entirely devoid of difficulty. Don't assume that, because you feel isolated, you are necessarily getting it wrong. Do make the time to think about it very, very carefully – to do otherwise would be arrogant and foolhardy – but understand that sometimes it is right to be unreasonable.

I once drove to Bristol to collect my wife from the Cancer Care Centre. I'd had a disappointing week at work, largely spent failing to persuade reluctant funders to back a new idea. It was a testing summer personally and professionally. Having a little time to reflect I stopped at the Clifton Suspension Bridge. It is an extraordinary feat of engineering, and truly beautiful. I read the plaque. Apparently, construction had been delayed for lack of funds. In fact it stopped altogether for several years whilst Brunel struggled and failed to find support for the project. He went away, built railways, dug tunnels, learnt, persuaded, inspired and eventually returned many years later to complete a modern miracle.

No matter how the rejection may make us feel, a brilliant idea doesn't stop being a brilliant idea just because we can't raise the cash for it or, more generally, because others cannot see what we can see.

Be unreasonable for as long as it takes.

(10) **HAVE A LAUGH** Amidst all these dire warnings it is easy to forget why we wanted to exercise leadership in the first place. The time when we stop enjoying the challenge will almost certainly be the time when we stop doing the job well.

The Community Links' Trustee Board was led from the beginning until March 2007 by a solicitor called Stanley Harris. Stan has done all our legal work for free, totalling, no doubt, tens of thousands of pounds worth of *pro-bono* service. He has also raised funds, introduced friends and chaired an awful lot of meetings, but I don't think any of these contributions have been as important as his enjoyment of a good joke.

Stan's ability to stay cheerful, to smile and encourage, to share a personal story, to bring sweets and drinks to the meeting, to be consistently and reliably positive in the most testing times has been, perhaps, the Trustees' greatest asset. It is, in my book, not only unconditional leadership. It is also great leadership. As Chair of Community Links, the leader of our organisation, Stan knows as well as anybody that not everything is perfect all the time. But he also understands, as very few do, that being miserable or demoralised or distant never improves anything. Stay cheerful, even when it's hard, because morale is important, because it gets results and because life is short.

(11) PERSEVERE Unconditional leadership is not colouring by numbers. It is painting your own picture. It is not leadership by rote or regulation. It is, on a good day, leadership that sings.

Persevere because …

'The days are not full enough.
And the nights are not full enough.
And life slips by like a field mouse
not shaking the grass.'

Ezra Pound

Go for it!

Being Something

DENNIS HEALEY recently advised Gordon Brown on the crucial difference between running the Treasury and running the country: 'Chancellors must do something' he said, 'Prime Ministers must *be* something'.

Pithy advice which captures, I think, the essential distinction between competent management and great leadership. It is a distinction which works not only for the high offices of state but for all shared endeavours, huge and tiny. Since completing the first edition of *Unconditional Leadership* I have been involved in three pieces of work which have further shaped my thinking.

Second, we have launched We Are What We Do, which I was working up as an idea and pitching to potential partners when working on the first edition. We Are What We Do has now published two best sellers – *Change The World For A Fiver* and *Change The World 9 to 5* and launched a variety of sparky endeavours all inspiring the small changes in attitudes and behaviour which can make a real difference if enough of us do the same thing. It's based on a very simple formula – small actions times lots of people equals big change (www.wearewhatwedo.org).

Third and most recently, I have been working with the new Prime

Minister Gordon Brown on the development and delivery of his vision for social action. In particular we have been working together on the development of a new Council on Social Action chaired by the Prime Minister acting, not as Manager of the Government, but as leader of the country.

These three apparently very different projects have been connected in my mind by several of the principles outlined in my vision of unconditional leadership – the idea that we can all do something, we can 'lead from the middle' and so create together something far greater than the sum of the parts. The belief that such an enterprise will only succeed if it is anchored on the firm ground of shared values, which are widely communicated and universally understood. And the conviction that this concept of leadership that we began to explore as a tiny £360 community project working from home thirty years ago might work equally well in Westminster and Whitehall.

Great leadership is, of course, in part about the things we do, otherwise it is just shallow rhetoric but it is also and essentially about what we are – 'being' and 'doing' in Lord Healey's cogent phrase, and the relationship between the two. We are what we do.

The Living Values Collaborative Enquiry was, for me, a particularly instructive experience. It has often been claimed that the distinguishing feature of organisations in the third sector is that they are value-driven, but the values of the sector as a whole have never been defined. We didn't set out to create a definitive list but we did want to test the casual assumption – are they really that important? The resulting Living Values report is too thorough and thoughtful to summarise effectively here. If you are interested in learning more please go to www.community-links.org for the download, but two findings were particularly striking and relevant to this readership:

> we can all do something, we can 'lead from the middle' and so create together something far greater than the sum of the parts

First, effective well-led organisations don't think of values as relevant only to planning or to marketing or to monitoring and measurement. They are present in ALL that they do.

Values are the beginning, they are what inspire us.

Values are the means; they are what we do and how we do it.

And values are the end they are what we strive to achieve.

Secondly, the enquiry followed up the often repeated lament that new funding streams, the demands of the market, political pressures etc placed difficult new demands on the sector and our values are thus under threat. Further investigation revealed that our values are indeed under threat but the threat comes not from external forces but rather from within.

It lies in organisations:

- Not focusing clearly on values
- Chasing funding that does not fit values
- Allowing values to be influenced by others outside the sector
- Allowing the demands of running an organisation to overshadow its values.

For me this work offered powerful new evidence to support the belief that values are not a touchy feely extra adorning the Annual Report or the website home page but rarely intruding on the real business of day-to-day management. They are at the heart of every successful organisation, in the heart of every successful leader.

Our work on this project focused on the third sector, but I have found that it also resonates very well with audiences from across the sectors. In the last couple of years we have undertaken training and I have made presentations focusing on values to audiences as diverse as the Department of Employment, the Fire Service, Pricewaterhouse, ICI and several local authorities. Many of these organisations were undergoing periods of rapid change, but all were embracing the Dalai Lama's advice to 'open your arms to change but never let go of your values'. The truth is universal – values are the bedrock.

If, however, this is widely recognised, my beliefs about risk are less generally shared. In particular, Government and public sector bodies struggle with the conviction that there can be no progress without risk and no risk without occasional failure. I understand that we each occupy a different place on the risk curve. I tried to make this point in chapter seven with my story about the Treasury official in the venture capital company, but if we are not prepared to entertain any form of risk we are closing the door also on any prospect of progress. In *The point of*

> **The more remote from the frontline we become the more important it is for leaders to consistently restate and occasionally reframe the value and purpose of the work**

Departure, former Foreign Secretary Robin Cook recalls an exchange with a very senior Civil Servant at a Cabinet sub-committee. The Foreign Secretary asked the Civil Servant what he was responsible for. The Civil Servant replied 'I am accountable for the validity of the reporting system'. It is an answer that reminded me of a game my three-year-old sister used to play. My parents were thinking of moving house and estate agents kept sending them lots of details of houses they couldn't afford. My sister arranged them on the kitchen table, scribbled on them, rearranged them, gabbled into her Mickey Mouse telephone and rearranged them again. She was, she said an 'Astid Igent' and it entertained her for hours.

I think there are still Astid Igents to be found in all sorts of organisations large and small, but most often in public sector bodies – hard-working conscientious people who are doing all the things that busy people do but not actually achieving anything. Efficient systems can create an illusion of productivity not actually producing anything, and the bigger an organisation becomes the easier it is to slip into these patterns of behaviour without either intending to do so or recognising that it has happened. For large organisation these may be big goals addressed over a sustained period – Ikea have ten targets for ten years – but they will always be goals to which everyone in the organisation must be capable of relating their day-to-day labour.

As we have moved on I have thought more about delegation and recruitment. I was struck by a survey conducted by Leadership IQ which showed that 46% of newly hired employees failed within eighteen months, while only 19% achieved unequivocal success. These were depressing figures but the coda was even more striking:

'While the failure rate for new hires is distressing it should not be surprising: 82% of managers reported that in hindsight the interview process with these employees elicited subtle clues that they will be headed for trouble. But during the interviews Managers were too focused on other issues, too pressed for time or lacked confidence in their interviewing abilities to heed the warning signs'.

Reflecting on those conclusions I realised how many times I had been there myself. The in tray is overflowing, the recruitment process has taken three months, the team are eager to welcome a new colleague, I am impatient to conclude the process and anyway the successful candidate looks good on points 1 to 3, does it really matter about point 4? The answer of course is, yes it does. It is far easier to prolong the recruitment process and keep searching until we find the right candidate than it is to address the difficult and sensitive issues involved in appointing the wrong person, restoring team morale and repairing the damage to the work. Bill Gates reportedly spends more than 80% of his time on recruitment. At first sight this seems like a disproportionate emphasis on one aspect of the business but on reflection we can see that if a leader can get this job right everything else falls into place. No amount of time spent on careful recruitment is disproportionate.

Re-reading the first edition of *Unconditional Leadership* reminded me of how much time we spent, particularly in the early days of Community Links, learning lessons the hard way and breaking new ground. I have been reflecting further on that. Sometimes it has taken us to a place where no-one has ever been before but sometimes we have merely created a new path where one was already well established.

In part this was because we didn't do our research, we just charged on. That was short-sighted but in part it was also a reasonable response to a culture which prizes innovation but places little value on effective replication. We create institutions and prizes and funding streams all dedicated to developing, supporting and celebrating successful innovation, but no equivalents for copying although surely there is limited point in a new idea if it is not effectively replicated. I was recently part of a judging panel for national awards recognising effective projects in the public sector. One scheme successfully fused two brilliant ideas, one from the US and one from Scotland. 'It's just copying' said one judge, his tone dripping with disdain. He was completely overlooking the main point which was, for me, the fact that it was a stunning success. Science fiction writer William Temple said 'the future is already here it is just unevenly distributed'. As brave and visionary leaders we should not assume that we have to find a new way of doing everything. It is our responsibility to find the best way and to encourage and support others to do the same. It may or may not be new.

Finally, our recent work has led me to reflect on scale. Earlier this year we worked with the Prime Minister on his book *Britain's Everyday Heroes*. It told the stories of ordinary people whose willing commitment

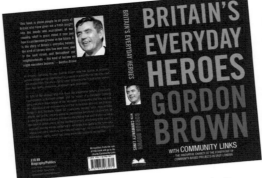

to a cause or a community had informed and inspired him – the woman who had been the inspiration behind community reconciliation in Northern Ireland and the leader of a campaign tackling gun culture in Manchester. The innovator transforming the way we use the internet as a tool for democracy and the campaigner who had established the world's first fair trade town. Councillors leading local regeneration efforts, public servants going far beyond the parameters of their job, a new generation of social entrepreneurs proving that successful business can benefit communities, creative pioneers who brought the arts to a deprived housing estate, gardening to refugees and opera to the homeless and carers, mentors, coaches and volunteers who gave themselves quietly every day, expecting neither praise nor recognition.

The range of stories reminded me that leadership comes in many shapes and forms. Some of these 'heroes' were leading large organisations, others were working on their own but all were, to paraphrase Roosevelt, doing what they could with what they've got from where they are.

They reminded me of a friend I first met in Tower Hill Gardens when I was a teenager. She talked to homeless people on the streets, full-time. Sometimes she shared rollups or sandwiches or a cup of tea from a thermos flask but mainly she made friends. Some of those friendships led years later down long and winding paths to jobs and permanent homes. To stability.

My friend died recently and suddenly, still young and full of life. 'She was truly something' said a mutual aquaintance.

> **leadership comes in many shapes and forms**

There are still homeless people on the streets, more perhaps than when she began, but she had saved a life or two. For all our status or our learning or our money how many left can say as much?

'Being something' – it is, above all, the quality of what we do and how we do it that that mark out the great, unconditional leader. Not the scale.

Editorial from the Times of India 16 Aug 2007

Take the Lead

As we celebrate the 60th anniversary of independence, it is appropriate that this newspaper should have initiated a campaign called Lead India, an exhortation to the country's youth to come forward and take the initiative in the enterprise of taking us through the 21st century, and beyond. Central to the Times of India's campaign is the concept of leadership and what it means – or ought to mean – in today's age of Internet, satellite television and other forms of digital democracy. In the past, when India has taken faltering steps towards its long-postponed tryst with destiny, the cry has gone up: 'What India needs is a strong leader'.

Today, more than ever, it is crucial to raise the question whether a country as populous and as diverse as ours can afford to have a strong leader, with the undertones of latent fascism that the term implies. Yet, India undeniably needs leadership. How is this seeming paradox to be resolved?

Perhaps the answer lies in redefining the concept of leadership. Once again, Mohandas Karamchand Gandhi comes to mind as an innovative exemplar of a leadership that was based not on command but on making oneself answerable to the dictates of one's conscience. Gandhi – who never sought or assumed political office – was the leader supreme because he understood that true leadership lies in empowering individuals to take charge of their own quests for life, liberty and the pursuit of happiness. Like true freedom, leadership is not something which is given but something which one earns.

Today, India is once more at the crossroads. In many ways it is 'the best of times and the worst of times'. The best, in that the country is an emerging economic and cultural superpower. The worst, that extreme, chronic poverty and social marginalisation coexist in cruel juxtaposition with our achievements. What is needed to tilt the balance in India's favour is leadership in the true sense. How can we together create a political and social space so that those who have so long been led can become leaders in their own right?

In a population of a billion plus there is vast and untapped human potential of talent and enterprise. The key lies in unleashing this long pent-up force. How do we collectively and individually do this? Not by leaving it to governments that believe that people are meant to be led and not to be leaders themselves. What we can, and must, do is to seek out individual initiatives and projects of successful leadership, which have transformed a corporate house or a community, and use these as inspirations to energise our own search for excellence. So take the lead. It is no one else's but yours to take.

Appendix 1

Community Links
– the background

Our Vision

To be champions of social change.

Our Purpose

To tackle the causes and consequences of social exclusion by developing and running first-rate practical activities in East London and by sharing the local experience with practitioners and policy-makers nationwide.

Our Work

Community Links has helped tens of thousands of children, teenagers, adults and older people in deprived neighbourhoods of east London for 30 years.

Many have faced difficult challenges. They may be struggling to make ends meet or to make a home in a new country. Some suffer from the consequences of being born into poverty – poor health, inadequate housing, loneliness and isolation. Others may just need some support to make life a little easier.

We run a network of over 60 community projects that empower individuals to build a brighter future; 80% of our staff live locally, many are former users of our services.

...we all have the potential to do great things

Our programme of national work shares the local lessons across the country to widen the impact of our projects and generate lasting social change;

Our Principal Activities

■ WITH CHILDREN AND YOUNG PEOPLE

Every child can succeed; some are denied the opportunity. Our projects include play schemes, after-school clubs, youth groups, at-risk groups, training programmes, crime-reduction programmes, supplementary education and detached youth work on the streets. In many cases former users of our services, including junior leaders, deliver our youth work.

■ WITH ADULTS

Every adult can build a ladder out of poverty. We provide the hammer and nails. Activities include advice, advocacy and home visiting services, training programmes, outreach to the elderly and our community development workers helping local groups build their capacity. Many of these services were delivered by people who first came to us as users themselves and have since taken one of our accredited training programmes.

■ OUR NATIONAL WORK

Community Links pioneers new ideas and new ways of working locally, we go on to share the learning nationally; generating practical social action in other communities and influencing national policy. Our national team, linksUK, shares the learning from our local work through policy development, publications, public speaking, training and consultancy … from the ground up.

Our Structure

Community Links is a registered charity founded in 1977. Our annual income of around £9.5 million is derived from government and statutory agencies, fundraising events, charitable trusts, corporate sponsors and other donors. We spend around 90% of our income directly on service delivery; we employ a permanent staff team of 185, and hundreds of volunteers are regularly involved.

Further information

Visit: www.community-links.org
Email: uk@community-links.org
Community Links 105 Barking Road, Canning Town, London E16 4HQ

Appendix 2

Community Links' CV

Our values

'To generate change. To tackle causes not symptoms, find solutions not palliatives. To recognise that we all need to give as well as to receive and to appreciate that those who experience a problem understand it best. To act local but to think global, teach but never stop learning. To distinguish between the diversity that enriches our society and the inequalities that diminish it. To grow – but all to build a network not an empire. To be driven by dreams, judged on delivery. To never do things for people but to guide ... and support, to train and enable, to simply inspire'.

Community Links tackles the causes and consequences of social exclusion by not only developing and running practical activities in East London but also by sharing the local experience with practitioners and policy-makers nationwide. Here are some of the results:

■ *'To generate change'*

Community Links' advice sessions on unsafe tower block estates in the 1980s inspired the Newham Tower Block Tenants Campaign. This became the outstanding direct action campaign of its time, forcing the demolition of the notorious Ronan Point in 1986 and leading to the birth of The

National Tower Blocks Directory ·1992·

National Tower Block Campaign and the demolition of similar dangerous buildings across the UK.

■ 'To tackle causes not symptoms'

In policy contributions from 1997 to 2000 we argued that local community groups, documented in our series of Ideas Annuals, were tackling child poverty effectively but on a small scale, and that the government needed to learn from these groups and to fund them.

In October 2000, the Chancellor announced the creation of the new £450 million Children's Fund, supporting local community groups tackling child poverty. The six examples in his presentation were all drawn from our Ideas Annuals. We went on to work in partnership with government on two publications featuring Children's Fund projects, which celebrate even the smallest community organisation's contribution to national policy target of reducing child poverty.

■ 'To find solutions not palliatives'

We constantly bring to the Minister's door the experience of the family at ours. Examples include:

> **Community Links' proposal to the DSS:** 'Benefit rules should be modified or clarified so that small advance payments made to cover volunteer expenses do not effect benefit entitlement'.

  Policy Announcement: *'The DSS will extend the current disregard of volunteer's reimbursed expenses in the calculation of benefits to include payments made in advance'.*

> **Community Links' proposal to the Department of Work and Pensions:** 'The 48 hour rule should be changed where its application impedes community and voluntary activity'.

  Policy announcement: *'We will relax the current rule that requires volunteers to be available to take up employment in 48 hours notice'.*

> **Community Links' proposal to the Home Office:** 'Costs of being active in the community, such as a criminal records check, should be covered by government'.

Policy Announcement: *'From August, voluntary organisations will not have to pay for criminal record checks'.*

■ 'To recognise that we need to give as well as to receive'

Our Youth Volunteer scheme offers training, skills and opportunities to young people. In return, we ask that they give us their local experience, their time and their energy. This is a great combination – we helped 18 year-old Terry Hawkins from Canning Town get a job but he still volunteers for us on Sundays. *'I had a nice upbringing but since leaving school I've had a colourful background, you know what I mean? It would be good to work with troubled young people as I have had similar experiences as them. I am doing a Sports Leadership course through our S-Team programme and I want to set up a football team and teach others, especially troubled youths. After all, everyone deserves a second chance'.*

> **Community Links is an outstanding example of what can be achieved when people come together in partnership**
>
> His Royal Highness, the Prince of Wales

■ 'To appreciate that those who experience a problem understand it best'

Our report *Building Innovation into Regeneration*, published by the Rowntree Foundation in 1998, stated, *'unless and until we can find new ways of using mainstream budgets to tackle multiple deprivation we will always be tinkering at the edges'* and explained how this might be achieved. In launching the National Strategy for Neighbourhood Renewal in 2000 Prime Minister Tony Blair said, *'the strategy harnesses the hundreds of billions of pounds spent by key government departments rather than relying on one-off regeneration spending'*. Our Everyday Innovators programme continues to equip people with the skills to bring about positive change in their own communities.

■ 'To act local but think global'

'We Are What We Do' – the movement inspiring people to use their everyday actions to change the world – began life as a project of Community Links. To date WAWWD have sold over one million copies of the *'Change the World...'* books which have been published in seven countries, registered over one million individual actions on the website www.wearewhatwedo.org, and begun to change behaviour through initiatives such as the 'I'm not a plastic bag' campaign.

■ 'To teach but never stop learning'

We started an alternative education programme in 1978 for 'truanters', eventually our project was recognised and financially supported by the Local Authority. This took a while but was so successful we went around the country teaching other authorities about it. We also listened to the concerns of local teachers that some primary school children were showing signs of difficulty in school, so we started earlier educational intervention.

■ 'To distinguish between the diversity that enriches society and the inequalities that diminish it'

Community Links' Evidence Paper 5 coined the phrase 'The Uncounted' to describe 'legal citizens denied the right of citizenship'. We concluded that the uncounted population in London is as large as the total population of Norwich. Our Ideas Annual *'Small Places Close to Home'* reported on the remarkable work going on across the UK with community projects working with or led by refugees and people seeking asylum; demonstrating the contribution and potential of this significant group. Our extensive research into the Informal Economy reveals people working

out of 'Need not Greed' – our findings have been published and shared with policy makers. Investigating the real lived-experiences of the people we work with provides the evidence which improves our recommendations for policy change.

■ 'To grow – but all to build a network not an empire'

Over the last eight years our national team linksUK has:

- worked with over 5,000 local people using our innovative 'Everyday Innovators' approach

- established a campaign network to continue influencing government policy about the informal economy in deprived neighbourhoods

- published over 30 books and reports based on our research including a partnership with the Prime Minister

- worked with organisations exploring their values by providing support and consultancy.
- succeeded in securing 12 national policy changes
- hosted seven government secondments
- and has successfully tested 11 ideas for improving delivery of local services.

■ 'To be driven by dreams, judged on delivery'

Newham has the highest levels of youth unemployment in the country. Despite this, our government contract for delivering a New Deal programme has been hailed as the best of its kind in London and second best overall in the UK, resulting in the extension of the contract. We now work with over 300 clients and achieve an 'into job' rate of over 50%.

Around 100 young people have joined our 'Education Otherwise' programme after being excluded from mainstream education. Over the past year 183 young people came through our doors, some staying for the full year, some quickly returning back to school. Those that stayed achieved 63 exam passes and for the first year ever, we started to see results in A to C GSCE grades. Most of our Year 11 leavers went on to college after lots of encouragement from staff. These young people came to us at risk of getting no qualifications at all but we offered them a second chance at education. We continue to get results.

■ 'To never do things for people, but to guide and support, to train and enable'

Auction My Stuff is a Community Links social enterprise which sells 'stuff' on eBay. We give unemployed young people the chance to get the skills, experience and, above all, confidence for work. Through structured work or volunteer placements and intensive coaching young people get the chance to regain control of their lives.

'...one of Britain's most inspiring community organisations'

David Cameron Leader:
Conservative party

■ *'To simply inspire'*

'Community Links were fundamental to the development of TimeBank. Indeed, they inspired and came up with the idea of people giving what they are passionate about as opposed to people giving their time because they feel it is their duty.

'During the last 20 years, the team at Community Links have inspired all aspects of my work and each and every charity I have founded is a tribute to them.'

Jane Tewson, Founder of TimeBank, Comic Relief, Charity Projects and Pilotlight.

Community Links' work inspires us all

Gordon Brown,
Prime Minster

Unconditional Leadership:
Presentations, Development and Training

The Community Links approach to leadership is rooted in 30 years experience of pioneering community work in east London. Unconditional Leadership is based on and driven by values, empowers and engages, supports creativity and innovation, inspires trust and builds teams that thrive.

We have developed a range of materials and experiences to share our learning. An Unconditional Leadership Development Programme can be tailored to meet the needs of your organisation and your people, and can include one or more of the following:

■ **Group Presentation:** Alongside the learning outlined in this book David Robinson also shares his insights and perspectives on leadership directly with audiences through personal presentations and keynote speeches to corporate, public and voluntary sector audiences.

 'truly inspirational... he delivers a very powerful experience for his audience' AON

 'Good storytellers are rare - story tellers who speak from their own experience are even rarer. David Robinson is that mixture of inspiration and humility that changes the way people think, and more importantly, the way they act.' Business in the Community

 'Head and shoulders above every other speaker' Inchcape UK

 'Your talk gave us a wake up call and has triggered wider debate on the whole concept of leadership culture'. ICI International Leadership Conference

■ **Development Day:** a leadership programme that will inspire your people, support them to reflect on their organisational and personal values, and develop new ways of working and leading. Powerful presentations from the people that we work with in east London will change the way you think about leadership, and practical activities will enable you to develop your skills and understanding.

■ **Unconditional Leadership:** Reconnecting Policy and Practice : a unique programme designed specifically for civil servants in partnership with the National School for Government, to learn about leadership alongside local residents, working together to improve both national policy and local public services.

■ **Exposure:** opportunities for short work placements at Community Links

To talk to us about a bespoke presentation or development programme for your senior executives, staff, annual conference or leadership programme, contact Geraldine Blake geraldine.blake@ community-links.org

Living Values: A report encouraging boldness in third sector organisations.

By Geraldine Blake, David Robinson And Matthew Smerdon

 Community Links carried out a Collaborative Inquiry into the values of the third sector. We found that there is a set of values that are meaningful to third sector organisations and which inspire people to work in the sector. Whilst these values are also present in the public and private sectors the way in which third sector organisations combine and prioritise these values is unique. The report also carries the warning that there are forces with the potential to change the values of the third sector.

Living Values contains:

■ inspiring examples of organisations putting their values into action

■ thought-provoking comment from sector practitioners

■ a toolkit of practical exercises to get people talking about values.

'A very interesting exercise happening at an excellent time' Nicolas Deakin, Chair of the influential Commission of the Future of the Voluntary Sector

'The sense of immediacy and authenticity makes for an unusually compelling read' Stephen Cook, Editor: Third Sector Magazine

The learning from our work on values has enabled us to offer consultancy and training to support organisations exploring their values and how they are delivered. For more information contact Geraldine Blake geraldine.blake@community-links.org

We Are What We Do:
inspiring people to use their everyday actions to change the world...

Originated by David Robinson, We Are What We Do is a new national movement which aims to inspire people to use their everyday actions to change the world. It is not another charity. It's not an institution. It's a movement.

This movement has to date produced two books each featuring fifty simple actions which can begin to change the way people think ... and the way we act. The books have been translated and published around the world and over one million copies have now been sold.

The project website is the place to get more details of the actions, find reports on progress and make your own suggestions for further ideas. www.wearewhatwedo.org

Making Links: 15 visions of Community

To mark Community Links' 30th anniversary we invited some friends to take a look with us at the state of our communities and, perhaps more importantly, where we are going. We asked a diverse group of contributors to consider the question, 'What do we mean by "Community"?'

Alongside a personal recollection of his upbringing by the **Prime Minister** and some thoughts about community building from the **Leader of the Opposition**, we hear from: Phil Beadle – former teacher of the year, on the role of community schools; 15 year old **Alex Loukos** – local youth ambassador to the Olympics, about the prospect of the 2012 games in London; Russell Davies on a community formed online; **Stafford Scott** considering leadership in black and minority ethnic communities; **Mohammed Nazam** – founder of a multi-faith music project; and Kevin Harris writing about the way community can be formed through shared activities in public spaces.

This collection provides powerful insights into the many ways we live together. Making Links is available from Community Links at £10.99 and can be ordered online at www.community-links.org or by telephone 020 7473 2270.

Classic Yoga

Vimla Lalvani

Classic Yo

ga

Vimla Lalvani

hamlyn

Course Three   **89**

Contents

First published in hardback in Great Britain in 1996
by Hamlyn, an imprint of Octopus Publishing Group Limited
2-4 Heron Quays, London E14 4JP

This paperback edition first published 1998

Reprinted 2000

Text © The Natural Therapy Company Limited 1998

Design © Octopus Publishing Group Limited 1996

Photographs © Octopus Publishing Group Limited 1996

NOTE
It is advisable to check with your doctor before embarking on any exercise
program. Yoga should not be considered a replacement for professional medical
treatment; a physician should be consulted in all matters relating to health and
particularly in respect of pregnancy and any symptoms which may require

ISBN paperback 0 600 59745 8
ISBN hardback 0 600 58892 0

A CIP catalogue record for this book is available from the British Library.

Printed in China by Toppan Printing Co., (H.K.) Ltd.

diagnosis or medical attention. While the advice and information in this book
are believed to be accurate and the step-by-step instructions have been devised to
avoid strain, neither the author nor the publisher can accept any legal
responsibility for any injury sustained while following the exercises.

Introduction

What is Yoga?

Many people want to know what yoga is and how it can help them. In this book I hope to explain classical yoga in a modern sense and to de-mystify the principles of yoga philosophy. The benefits of yoga are many and people who practice regularly will see a great change in their physical body and their whole mental outlook.

Given the stresses and strains of our daily lives, we must learn the art of shutting ourselves away from

chaos and retreating into our inner selves to find peace, balance and harmony. Yoga teaches you how to achieve this. *Classic Yoga* explains how yoga can improve your everyday life. You will discover the real you and experience 'yoga living'. You will learn the techniques of yoga and understand the mental and physical aspects of the philosophy.

In Sanskrit, the word 'yoga' means the union of mind and body. Yoga is not a religion but a philosophy of life. It is an ancient science of movement developed in India thousands of years ago to improve all aspects of your life, both mental and physical. The main principle of yoga is that mastery over the mind and senses will lead to a cessation of misery and bring you salvation.

The Paths of Yoga

There are five different forms of yoga and for maximum benefit they should be practiced together. The four mental yogas are Bhakti yoga (emotions), Gyana yoga (wisdom), Raja yoga (meditation) and Karma yoga (actions). The one physical yoga is called Hatha yoga. In

'masculine' or 'feminine' are largely shared by men and women, it is essential that both energies are balanced equally. Yoga is the art and science of balance in everyday living and moderation in all that we do. It teaches us how to have harmonious relationships with others and how to understand our own inner truth. It connects us to our souls and sets us on a path of true spirituality. The ultimate goal for the yogi is to join the spiritual self to the cosmic energy of the universe.

this book we concentrate on Hatha yoga because it is the first stage of development; yoga philosophy states that before you can have a disciplined mind you must first begin to train your body.

Hatha yoga is a series of asanas, or postures, that train and discipline the body and mind. In Sanskrit, 'ha' means the sun or male energy and 'tha' the moon or female energy. When you practice the asanas you are combining and balancing the masculine and feminine energies which are within all of us, whether male or female. In the Western world today, where professions, tasks and hobbies that were once considered exclusively

Hatha Yoga

Hatha yoga exercises the glands, organs and nerves in the body as well as toning the muscles. The yoga exercises are divided between asanas (exercise positions), Pranayama (breath control), Raj asanas (meditative postures), and Nauli, Mudras and Bandhas (purifying and cleansing postures). The exercises might appear strange when you first begin but as you familiarize yourself with the sequences you will understand how they work. Fluid movements unblock energy and, combined with correct breathing, increase your vitality and discipline your mind.

Yoga for Today

The popularity of yoga has soared in recent years. Attitudes to health, spirituality, lifestyle and mankind's place in the environment have changed dramatically and people are seeking solutions to the problems of their everyday existence. In these confusing times, the environment is struggling for survival and we are suffering from mental and physical stress, with some new diseases making an appearance and old ones thought to have been conquered by antibiotics reasserting themselves. We cannot always change these

The Physical Benefits of Yoga

Yoga is totally different from other types of exercise. First of all, it is non-competitive. The purpose of yoga is to understand yourself through your yoga practice and to work slowly and deliberately to gain flexibility as you progress. It is the antithesis of the 'no pain, no gain' philosophy. Graceful, fluid movements replace pounding flesh, creating a balance and strength of the mind, body and spirit.

The purpose is not to build muscle but to build muscle tone. In yoga asanas the muscles are stretched

conditions but we can learn to cope with them. Yoga provides a perfect solution because it brings harmony and balance to your life; because your mental state is balanced you will be able to solve problems calmly and rationally, and because your physical health is improved you will have a better resistance to illnesses.

The yoga system is based on universal truths, so it does not interfere with anyone's religious beliefs. Yoga is for men and women of all ages and occupations and you can begin to learn at any time. Everyone's life is transformed and enriched by a new outlook, improved health, a new awareness and a fresh philosophy.

lengthwise. Fat is eliminated around the cells and, combined with correct breathing, the exercises will improve the circulation and release toxin build-up. This process will reduce cellulite.

Yoga asanas also regulate the metabolism which controls weight gain and loss. As we grow older the metabolism slows down automatically. Continued practice of yoga postures keeps the metabolism rate stable so your weight will not fluctuate, and you will be able to maintain your ideal weight. Yoga also builds the immune system, so you will rarely experience even a common cold, and exercises the internal organs so that the body will work like a finely tuned car which runs in peak condition.

Yoga also helps to ease physical tensions through deep stretching and correct breathing techniques. Working on the physical body with deep concentration on breathing creates a real and lasting sense of harmony, embracing the body and mind. Yoga is a wonderful way of learning how to relax. The physical techniques create a calm and concentration that extend beyond the body deep into the mind, effectively reducing stress at all levels.

Many people are quite content to continue with Hatha yoga and benefit from the new-found discipline. Others discover a need to go further. Yoga opens the mind to a certain stillness and clarity and many people find they wish to pursue a spiritual path. Yoga raises the conscious level and brings the soul, mind and body into union by means of eight disciplines: Yama (ethics); Niyama (religious observances); Asana (postures); Pranayama (breathing exercises) Pratyahara (withdrawal of senses from objects); Dharana (concentration); Dhyana (meditation); Samadhi (superconsciousness).

Diet and Lifestyle

Many people believe that in order to begin studying yoga they must change their habits. They may well fear that they will be told to give up meat, alcohol and smoking overnight! In fact, yoga is not about abstinence at all – rather, it is about the art of moderation.

In yoga, there are no fixed rules laid down about what is permissible. However, because the philosophy is about returning your body to its natural equilibrium you will not feel the need for excesses. When your mind and body are in harmony and you are in tune with yourself you will want to maintain a healthy, balanced lifestyle.

The Chakras

In the Sanskrit language, the word 'chakra' means 'wheel'. Chakras are 'wheels' that radiate energy in a circular motion through the vital centres of the spine. Just as antennae are able to pick up radio waves and transform them into sound, so chakras pick up cosmic vibrations and distribute them throughout the body via these energy centers.

In the spine we have seven chakras or energy centers moving from the tail bone up to the top of the head. Each center controls different senses, and all these centers must flow freely to maintain good health.

Many people have blocked chakras, and yoga exercises unblock them. The twisting and turning of the body stretches the nerves and the increased supply of oxygen cleanses and purifies the bloodstream. Every cell is renewed and the energy flows smoothly.

I like to use a hosepipe as an analogy. When there is a kink in the pipe the water will trickle out slowly and unevenly; when the pipe is unkinked the water will flow strongly. It is exactly the same in the case of energy. When the chakras are unblocked the energy flow will be powerful and dynamic.

Clasp your hands over your head and continue to stretch your arms up while keeping your knees and shoulders down. Feel your fingertips tingling with energy and release your hands in a sudden burst. You will be surprised at how energized and powerful you feel as a result of carrying out this simple exercise.

All yogic exercises are based on a formula of stretching, relaxation and deep breathing to increase the circulation and improve concentration. In the meditative poses, sitting while breathing deeply reduces the metabolic rate. When the body is kept in this steady

It is important for you to be able to visualize the energy moving through your spine and there is a technique that will allow you to experience this. Sit upright on the floor, preferably in a cross-legged or lotus position. Look over your surroundings, close your eyes and relax the muscles of your face. Begin to breathe deeply and slowly. Become aware of the energy in the base of your spine. Feel bliss, calm and serenity. Stretch your arms out to the sides of your body with your palms facing upward. Gradually raise your arms and visualize the energy slowly moving to the center of your spine, then between the shoulder blades, up through the base of your neck and on through to the very top of your head.

pose for some time, the mind becomes free of physiological disturbances caused by physical activity. There is a steady flow of nerve energy that electrifies the body and awakens the spiritual power in man through breathing techniques and concentration. The Raj asanas prepare you for meditation – focusing your mind on one thought. It is a scientific approach that you can apply to many areas of your life. When you rid your mind of useless thoughts, clarity is increased and you can find your own solutions rather than relying on a third party. This is one of the goals of the aspiring yogi. You will experience the power and joy of yoga when you can master your own thoughts and actions.

How to Use This Book

For this book I have specifically designed three yoga courses which are based on different levels of fitness and experience of yoga. The main objective of the book is to teach you the basics of yoga and to guide your progress through to Course 3. Before you begin Course 1, it is important that you become familiar with the safety guidelines (page 12), breath control (page 13) and correct posture (page 14). Before embarking on any course you should follow the warm-up (page 16) and cool down afterward with a relaxation routine (page 22).

suppleness. As you move into the more challenging yoga asanas you will feel a sense of elation in your ability to tackle these difficult poses; you will become energized and motivated, yet your mood will be calm.

The real challenge begins in Course 3, because the exercises combine the need for balance along with physical strength and stamina. They will show you immediately what your mental state is – some days you will be surprised by your skill and other days you will need a sense of humor! As you are different every day, so your yoga practice will be too; the most important

Course 1 is a foundation course in which you will learn the importance of breathing correctly and of aligning the spine. The yoga exercises are very gentle, slow and easy to follow, and will teach you to move in a new way. These exercises are linked with a specific breathing pattern which will allow your energy to alter and flow freely through the system. Keep your mind focused on what your body is doing as you are practicing them and try to maintain a calm frame of mind.

When you are sure you have thoroughly mastered Course 1 you can then move on to Course 2. This course presents you with more dynamic exercises which, you will quickly discover, call for more strength, stamina and

aspect to bear in mind is never to become discouraged.

You will probably find that you are able to do some asanas better on one side than the other. This is because our natural energy differs and some people are happier doing grounding exercises while others like to fly. The rule here is to try to do each asana equally well and to concentrate especially on those that you find difficult. In fact, when you experience difficulty it means that the area is weak and requires balancing. Yoga is a discipline, so only continued practice will show results. The results will be dynamic: an invigorated body, increased stamina, improved muscle tone and a feeling of total harmony and calm.

Explanation of Terms Used in This Book

◆ For first position, stand tall in perfect posture with your feet together.

◆ For second position, stand tall in perfect posture with your feet apart, directly under the hip bones, and toes pointing forward. If an exercise calls for wide second position, place your feet 1–1.2m (3–4ft) apart.

◆ To center yourself, concentrate on the solar plexus while breathing deeply. This helps to balance your physical and mental state.

◆ To lift your spine, concentrate on the tail bone (the coccyx) while lifting your spine straight.

◆ To open the chest, push your shoulder blades down and lift the chest naturally to create a positive outlook.

◆ If an exercise calls for a flat back, your spine should be straight and parallel to the floor.

◆ Lotus position: the classic posture for meditation and pranayama. Sitting with your spine erect, bend your knees and cross your ankles in front of you.

For the half lotus, pull one foot up high onto the opposite thigh and place the second foot under the thigh of your first leg.

For the full lotus, place the second leg over the first, with the foot high on the opposite thigh and your knees touching the floor.

The half lotus can also be assumed in a standing position and the full lotus can be performed sitting, or in the head and shoulder stands.

Safety guidelines

Here are some important guidelines which must always be followed in order to make sure that you are able to gain all the benefits that yoga has to offer and do not inadvertently injure yourself by exercising incorrectly.

◆ The yoga courses in this book have been designed for people who are in a normal state of health. As is the case with any fitness program, if you feel unfit or unwell or you are recovering from an illness or injury, are pregnant, have high blood pressure or suffer from any medical disorder you must consult your doctor before embarking upon any of the exercises.

Always follow the course exactly and do the exercises in the right order, and always begin your practice with the warm-up to help loosen the muscles. Exercising stiff muscles leads to injury.

◆ Never rush the movements and follow the directions exactly. Do not jerk your body and stop immediately if you experience any sharp pain or strain to any muscle.

Never push yourself and always do the pose only to your own capability. Remember that yoga is strictly non-competitive and, if you are following these courses with a friend, don't succumb to the temptation to go at the same rate of progress as him or her if it doesn't suit you. It is for you to find your own pace.

◆ Pay particular attention to your breathing in order to help relax and focus your mind. Pay special attention to your posture, too, and make sure that you always stand, sit or kneel upright (see pages 16–17).

When you are carrying out a standing exercise you will often be required to balance upon one leg. Keep the leg on which you are standing straight by lifting the muscle above the kneecap. Do not hyper-extend the knee because this can cause injury.

◆ Do not exercise on a full stomach. You must wait four hours after a heavy meal or one hour after a light snack.

◆ Choose a warm, quiet, well-ventilated place in which to exercise. Wear clothing that you can comfortably stretch in. All yoga exercises are done in bare feet so that you can grip the floor with your toes. You might need a mat for the floor work, but otherwise just make sure you exercise on an even, non-slip surface.

◆ After exercising, the body always needs a cooling down period to return it to normal. Always finish with the relaxation pose, even if just for a short time. However, the longer the relaxation period you can manage the better as deep breathing restores the equilibrium and calms the nervous system.

◆ Whenever you practice yoga, remember these basic principles: soul/mind control of movements; awareness of postures and movements; slow and deliberate movements; relaxation during movements; positive non-competitive attitude; go only as far as is comfortable.

Breathing

Learning the art of correct breathing is vital to your health and well-being. In yoga we breathe from the diaphragm. If you watch a baby breathe you can see the diaphragm rise and fall, but adults tend to breathe from the chest. When you breathe correctly you increase lung capacity and send more oxygen into the bloodstream, revitalizing and purifying the internal organs. Correct breathing acts as a natural tranquillizer to the nervous system; the deeper you breathe the calmer your mind becomes. Keep the breath even and always breathe through the nose, never the mouth unless specifically instructed.

1

Stand in perfect posture (see page 14). Inhale deeply and push your stomach out from the diaphragm. Do not move your chest, and keep your shoulders down.

2

Exhale deeply. Keep your breathing steady and even. Repeat Steps 1 and 2 for at least 10 full breaths. Always follow this breathing pattern before you start your yoga practice, to steady your mind.

Posture

One of the basics of yoga is to sit and stand in perfect posture, and many poses are designed to strengthen the muscles in the lower back so that you are able to lift your spine in perfect alignment. Whether you are sitting, standing or kneeling, think of a string pulling you up from the crown of your head. Always 'open the chest' by pushing your shoulder blades down, lifting the chest naturally. The basic standing pose is called Tadasana, which means 'the mountain'. It is a dynamic pose and you should be aware of every muscle in the body. Stand with your feet together and your weight evenly distributed between your toes and heels. Pull your stomach in, tuck your buttocks under and lift the muscle above the kneecaps. Keep your arms at your sides, elbows straight and fingertips together. To test yourself, balance on your toes; you should not fall backward or forward.

1

Stand tall with your feet firmly planted on the ground and your weight evenly distributed between your toes and heels. Keep your shoulders down and your stomach and tail bone pulled in.

-2-

*Sitting cross-legged, lift
your spine as far as you
can. This will center your
balance and create a
positive mental attitude.*

-3-

*Sit on your heels and place
your hands on your knees.
Now raise your spine,
straightening your elbows.*

Warm-Up

It is always essential to warm up the body slowly and gently before beginning the yoga course of your choice. This series of movements combined with breathing in the correct manner will help to loosen the spine and gently prepare your body for the other exercises that follow. Before you begin, focus attention on yourself and breathe deeply from your diaphragm for ten seconds. 'Center' – that is, focus on balancing your physical and mental state – by assuming a good posture. You need to stand evenly with your weight balanced between your toes and heels. As you do the exercises you will feel the energy flow freely from one movement to the next.

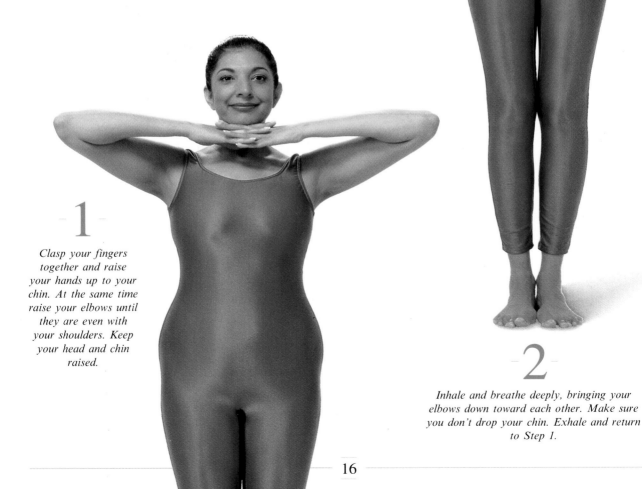

1

Clasp your fingers together and raise your hands up to your chin. At the same time raise your elbows until they are even with your shoulders. Keep your head and chin raised.

2

Inhale and breathe deeply, bringing your elbows down toward each other. Make sure you don't drop your chin. Exhale and return to Step 1.

3

Drop your head back, raise your elbows and clasp your hands under your chin.

4

Inhale and breathe deeply, bringing the elbows together. Exhale and return to Step 3.

5

Bring your clasped hands down, inhale and then raise your arms above your head and exhale.

7

Put your arms down by your sides, then inhale and stretch your left arm over to the right, keeping the hips square. Exhale and stretch downward, extending the right hand toward the floor. Continue inhaling and exhaling and stretch in both directions for 5 seconds. Then repeat on the other side.

6

Keep your chin up and shoulders down as you stretch your spine fully by reaching your arms as high as possible. Slowly inhale and exhale.

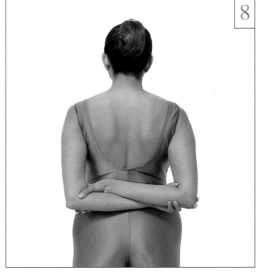

Put your arms behind your back and hold firmly
onto your elbows with your opposite hand. Slowly
inhale and exhale.

-10-

Exhale and lean forward so that your
back is flat. Keep your spine straight and
your chin forward.

-11-

Still exhaling and pointing with
your chin, lean over to a 45° angle,
keeping the spine straight as you
bend forward.

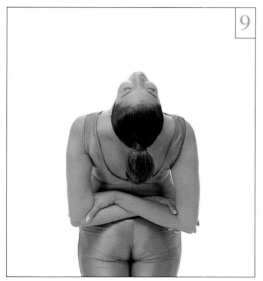

Inhale, push your hips forward and drop your head back, transferring your weight toward your heels. Keep your toes on the ground.

-13-

Inhale deeply and extend your arms out in front with your palms together and thumbs crossed. Keep your elbows straight and your arms close to your head. Inhale and exhale for 5 seconds.

12

Bend your knees to relax them and drop your head down toward your knees, letting your arms drop to the floor. Relax your spine, and continue to breathe steadily for 5 seconds.

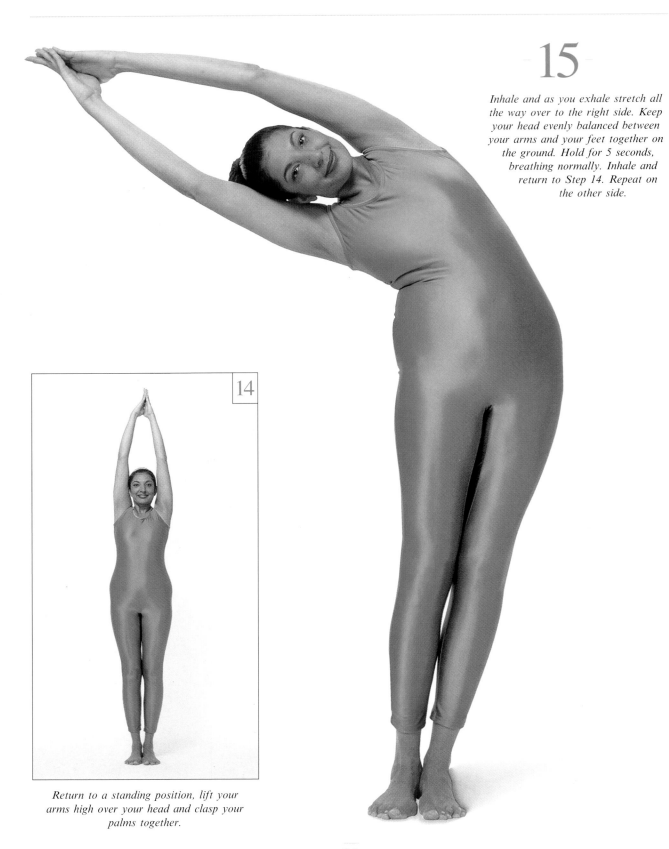

15

Inhale and as you exhale stretch all the way over to the right side. Keep your head evenly balanced between your arms and your feet together on the ground. Hold for 5 seconds, breathing normally. Inhale and return to Step 14. Repeat on the other side.

14

Return to a standing position, lift your arms high over your head and clasp your palms together.

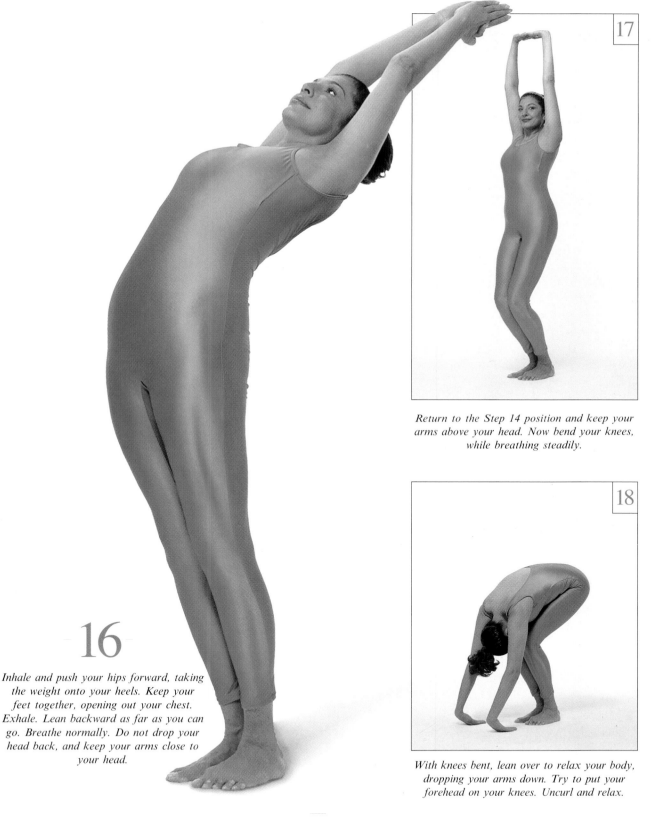

17

Return to the Step 14 position and keep your arms above your head. Now bend your knees, while breathing steadily.

18

With knees bent, lean over to relax your body, dropping your arms down. Try to put your forehead on your knees. Uncurl and relax.

16

Inhale and push your hips forward, taking the weight onto your heels. Keep your feet together, opening out your chest. Exhale. Lean backward as far as you can go. Breathe normally. Do not drop your head back, and keep your arms close to your head.

Relaxation

Learning the art of relaxation is essential to your well-being. These techniques not only help to rejuvenate the body but also release stress and tension in the muscle groups and calm the nerves. If you use the breathing exercise in the middle of the day it will refresh your mind and body. If you do it at night before you go to sleep, it can help cure insomnia. To release stress and tension in the muscle groups, begin by first focusing on your diaphragm and breathe deeply and slowly for 15 seconds. On every exhalation you'll feel the tension release from your body. Concentrate your mind on a pleasant image, such as a beautiful beach. Now concentrate on your feet and tense and release your toes. Flex your feet hard and as you relax them you'll feel the tension release in your ankles, knees, thighs, buttocks and stomach muscles. Repeat with your hands, tightening the arms and elbows while gripping your hands in a tight fist. Now raise your shoulder blades up and then relax them down again. Repeat twice. Next turn your head slowly to the right and slowly to the left, then let your head flop down. Finally, relax the face muscles, breathing deeply and keeping calm.

-1-

This is the dead man's pose. Lie flat on the floor with the palms of your hands facing upward and make sure your feet and legs are relaxed. Stay in this position for 15 minutes for the maximum benefit.

COURSE ONE

Course 1 is a foundation course for total beginners. It will teach you to balance your mental and physical energies and increase your flexibility and muscle tone, while improving your body shape and relaxing your nervous system.

Yoga is a science of movement: you should always begin with the Warm-up (page 16), and the exercises must be followed in

their exact order. In Course 1 you are introduced slowly to the system with easy poses and stretches which will familiarize you with the yoga way of movement; you should pay special attention to details like hand and feet positions.

Remember that even when you do not feel as if you are moving, yoga is never static. Modern physical exercises like aerobics

require a lot of energy, as every violent move burns it up; lactic acids are formed in the muscle fibers and this tires the muscles. The slow movements of yoga waste no energy; deep breathing allows more oxygen absorption and muscles suffer no fatigue.

Concentrate on what your body is doing. This is the first step toward disciplining the mind and body.

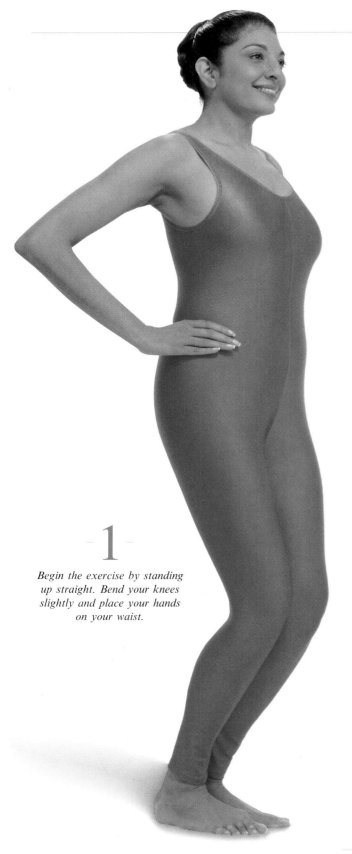

Head to Knee

This Head to Knee exercise lengthens the spine forward and is an excellent way to increase your body's flexibility and release unwanted body toxins. It helps soothe the nervous system, and will also relax the brain. You should never force your body forward, but as you increase the depth of your breathing you will be able to ease into the joy of deep stretching. It is very important to stretch forward from the waist. At the same time keep your back flat and don't round your shoulders. You might feel a pull in your hamstrings or some stiffness in the lower back. If this happens and you feel a bit dizzy, stretch your spine forward halfway, put your palms on a wall and keep your feet slightly apart.

1

Begin the exercise by standing up straight. Bend your knees slightly and place your hands on your waist.

2

Inhale and throw your arms forward, putting your head down between your arms. Bend your knees deeper and keep your head in line with your back.

Exhale and then throw your arms out straight behind your back, in line with your shoulders, but still keep your body in the same bent position.

Take your hands down and hold your ankles from behind, moving your head down toward your knees. Breathe normally for 5 seconds.

5

Now straighten your knees as much as you can. Pull your stomach muscles in, and drop your head down to your knees. Hold this position for at least 5 to 10 seconds. You'll feel the energy flow in a circular motion from your toes up the spine to your head. Uncurl and relax.

Dog Pose

This exercise is wonderful for stretching the whole body. Not only does it increase blood circulation, it also helps to tone and strengthen the legs and arms as well as curing fatigue and increasing your vitality. As with all the downward poses, it calms the nervous system and can be used as a relaxation pose if you're tired. Breathe deeply and evenly throughout the movements and relax your neck to release any tension in the shoulders.

1

Sit back on your heels with your toes curled under. Stretch out your arms in front of you and straighten your elbows. Place your forehead on the floor.

2

Inhale and kneel up, keeping your hands balanced out in front of you. Exhale and breathe normally. Stretch your fingers evenly on the floor, and keep your knees under the hips.

4

Now flatten your heels on the floor and move your thighs outward. Lift up your knees and stretch your spine upward. Straighten your arms and keep your shoulders down. Relax your face and neck, and breathe deeply for 30–60 seconds. As you gain flexibility, hold for longer. Relax and slowly stand upright.

3

Inhale, push the palms down and raise your hips upward. Stretch high onto your toes, pushing the shoulder blades down. Open out the chest and release the neck and shoulders. Bring your head in line with your spine and push your hips back. Hold for 10 seconds, while breathing normally.

The Tree

This standing pose focuses your mind and helps you learn how to concentrate and balance steadily on one leg. By balancing properly, you challenge your mind and you can unite your mental and physical energies. It also teaches you the importance of distributing your weight evenly between your heels and toes.

3

Now stretch your arms right up, while holding your balance for 5 seconds. Feel the energy move from your heels through your legs, into the spine and then through your arms and fingertips. Repeat on the other side.

1

Stand up straight. Place your right foot on your inner left thigh or close to the ankle or knee. Push out your hip but keep your hips square. Place your left hand on your left hip. Lift your standing leg as high as possible by stretching the muscle above the kneecap.

2

Look straight ahead and try to balance comfortably. When you are absolutely still, place your palms together and hold for 5 seconds. Grip the floor firmly with your toes so that the ankle does not move from side to side.

Side Stretch

Stretching to the side is an exercise that improves every muscle, joint, tendon and organ in the body. It also revitalizes the nerves, veins and body tissue by increasing the flow of oxygen to the blood. It helps cure sciatica, lumbago and other lower-back ailments. The body's strength and flexibility is heightened by the deep stretching, especially in the hip joints, waist and torso.

1

Stand up straight and place your feet about 1m (3ft) apart. Stretch out your arms with your palms facing down. Keep them in line with your shoulders. Breathe normally.

2

Turn in your left foot slightly and point your right foot 90° to the right. Inhale and stretch to the right. Keep the spine straight and do not tilt forward. Breathe normally and hold for 5 seconds.

3

Place your right hand on your right ankle and extend your left arm up in a straight line with your palm facing forward. Look up toward your arm, keeping your head up. Relax your face and shoulders, and hold for 10 seconds.

▶

4

Take the left arm over and bend to the right to feel the additional stretch. Turn your head forward and keep your weight on your back heels to maintain an equal stretch on both sides of the torso. Hold for 5 seconds.

5

Return to Step 1. Bring your arms to your sides, placing your right arm on your right leg. Kneel on your left knee. Stretch the right leg out, pointing the toes. Balance evenly.

6

Inhale deeply and stretch out the right leg as far as possible without tilting forward. Stretch your left arm over to the right and feel the pull in your side. Keep your head balanced between your arms. Exhale and breathe normally.

7

Now sit on the floor, stretch out your right leg and fold your left leg in front, placing your foot on your inner right thigh. Clasp your right hand around your right foot and flex your thumb. Bend your right elbow and stretch forward toward the knee.

SIDE STRETCH

8

Inhale, take your left arm over your head and try to reach your right thumb with your fingers. Keep turning your upper torso to the side and keep your head evenly balanced. Increase the stretch and hold for 5 seconds.

9

Exhale and relax your head and arms down over your right knee. Keep your right foot flexed and, as you breathe normally again, relax your body further down toward the floor.

10

Lift your head up and stretch your legs out as wide as possible. Inhale and as you exhale stretch forward with your arms to reach your heels, or just reach for your thighs, knees or ankles. Stretch with your spine straight. Breathe deeply and hold for 10 seconds.

11

Now relax your head down toward the floor. Stretch your arms out, while keeping the toes flexed. Breathe normally and turn your knees upward, but push down. Hold for 15 seconds. Repeat on the other side.

The Warrior

The Warrior pose is dynamic in its approach, and its aim is to develop a positive mental attitude and to give you physical control over your body. The Warrior is the basis for all standing postures, so the exact positioning of your spine, arms, legs and feet is very important. Hold your spine very straight as you open out your chest.

1

Stand up straight, feet together, and bend your knees slightly in preparation to jump. Bring your arms up to shoulder level and place your fingertips together.

2

Jump to open your legs wide – they should be about 1.2m (4ft) apart. Make sure your toes are pointing forward and stretch both your arms out sideways.

3

Turn your right knee and foot to the right. Lean your body backward and push your hips and stomach forward. Now bend your right knee, keeping your spine straight. Bend further until there is a 90° angle between your thigh and the floor. Repeat on the other side.

Side Twist

The standing twist helps to tone the leg muscles and waist, as well as relieving back pain and other ailments such as sciatica and lumbago. The twisting motion invigorates the abdominal organs and releases any toxins from the system. Remember to keep both legs straight as you twist from the hip upward.

1

Stand upright with your feet about 1.2m (4ft) apart and your toes pointing forward. Hold your arms out level with your shoulders and stretch out as far as you can.

2

Now turn sideways to the left, pointing out your left foot. Make sure your heel is in line with the right foot's instep. Still keep your arms outstretched.

3

Now hold your left ankle with your right hand and look over your left shoulder. Keep your arms in a straight line. Hold for 10 seconds and then repeat on the other side. Breathe normally throughout.

Sitting Twist

If you practice these twisting movements
regularly, any pain that you are suffering in your
lower back will rapidly diminish. The muscles
of your neck will also be strengthened,
especially when you look over the shoulder (not
shown) and any tension is released from your
spinal system. Your liver and spleen are
activated by the movements and the size of your
abdomen is reduced in the twisting position.

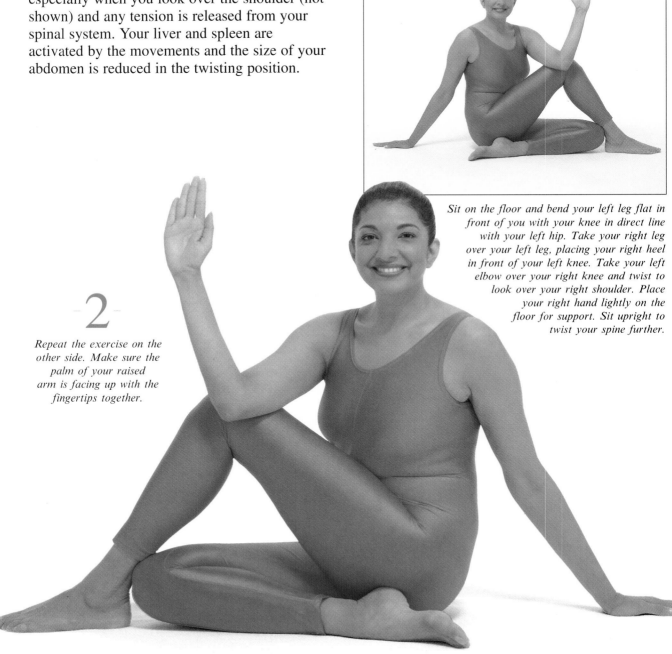

*Sit on the floor and bend your left leg flat in
front of you with your knee in direct line
with your left hip. Take your right leg
over your left leg, placing your right heel
in front of your left knee. Take your left
elbow over your right knee and twist to
look over your right shoulder. Place
your right hand lightly on the
floor for support. Sit upright to
twist your spine further.*

2

*Repeat the exercise on the
other side. Make sure the
palm of your raised
arm is facing up with the
fingertips together.*

Toe Pull

This Toe Pull exercise stretches the body forward from the hips, helps to strengthen the leg muscles and increases the flexibility of the hamstrings and the spine. The movement stimulates the kidneys, liver and pancreas as you pull in the abdominal muscles. It also helps to flatten the stomach.

Sit upright with your legs out in front of you. Flex both feet and raise your arms over your head. Hold onto your elbows, keeping your shoulders down. Breathe normally.

Bend forward from the hips, keeping the back flat. Try not to curve your spine. Hold up your chin, keeping your head balanced between your arms. Hold for 5 seconds.

Reach further forward and try to grasp two fingers around your big toes. Flex the thumbs and keep the elbows straight. Inhale and exhale, and hold for 5 seconds.

Bend your elbows and stretch forward, pointing your chin. Keep your back flat and your head out in front. Breathe deeply and hold for 10 seconds.

Leg Pull

This exercise improves the flexibility of the leg muscles and also helps to tighten the abdominal muscles. The lower back is strengthened, and the movements help to give you good balance. Sit upright as much as possible to avoid rolling over to one side.

1

Lie balanced on your side, leaning on your left elbow. Make sure your elbow is directly under your shoulder blade. Point your toes.

2

Inhale and bend your right knee in at a 90° angle to your left leg. Take hold of your big toe with your right hand and flex your thumb. Exhale.

3

Inhale and straighten your right leg to make a 90° angle with your left leg, flexing the toes. Breathe normally and hold for 5 seconds. Relax the leg down and repeat on the other side.

Flat Twist

The Flat Twist relieves any tension that gets trapped in the neck and shoulders. It also alleviates lower back pain and is a really good stretching exercise for your spine. Remember to keep both shoulders flat on the ground and always look in the opposite direction to your feet to increase the body stretch.

1

Lie flat on the ground and take your arms out to the side, placing your palms facing down. Put your left heel on top of the toes of the right foot. Breathe normally.

2

Inhale and as you exhale twist both feet to the right and look over your left shoulder. Hold the position for 5 seconds.

3

Bend your knees into your chest to increase the stretch, keeping legs and feet together. Inhale as your legs come up and then exhale and twist to the left. Relax onto your back and repeat on the other side.

Leg Lifts

These exercises will tone your stomach and leg muscles and improve the flexibility of your hamstrings and spine. It might be quite difficult in the beginning to achieve Step 3, but with continued practice you will be able to release all the stiffness in your joints.

Lie on the floor. Clasp your hands behind your left knee and bring it into your chest. Lift your head up from the floor toward the knee. Point your toes and lift your right leg just off the floor. Breathe normally and hold for 5 seconds.

Put your hands around your ankle, if you can, and stretch further, trying to place your forehead on your knee. Trying to keep both legs straight and breathing normally, hold for 10 seconds. Repeat Steps 1 and 2 on the other side.

3

Clasp your fingers around your big toe and pull your right leg even further toward your head, keeping your right foot flexed. Take your left arm out, with your palm facing down, and hold just above your left leg. Breathe deeply, hold for 10 seconds and repeat on the other side.

The Fish

When you do the Fish exercise you'll tone the stomach and leg muscles as well as releasing tension in the neck and shoulders. It also improves circulation to the face and slows the ageing process. These movements strengthen the lower back and open out the chest, increasing your lung capacity, which improves conditions such as bronchitis and asthma.

Lie on the floor with your arms out and point your toes. Inhale and raise your chest, resting your weight on the crown of your head. Feel the stretch in your neck and face. Exhale and breathe normally, holding for 3 seconds.

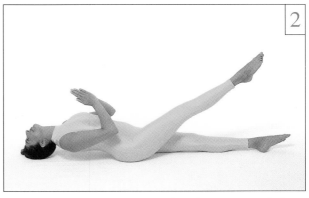

Still balancing on your head, inhale and raise your right leg, keeping your hip on the floor. Place your palms together above your chest, holding for 3 seconds. As you exhale, lower your leg slowly. Relax to the floor, if necessary, before Step 3.

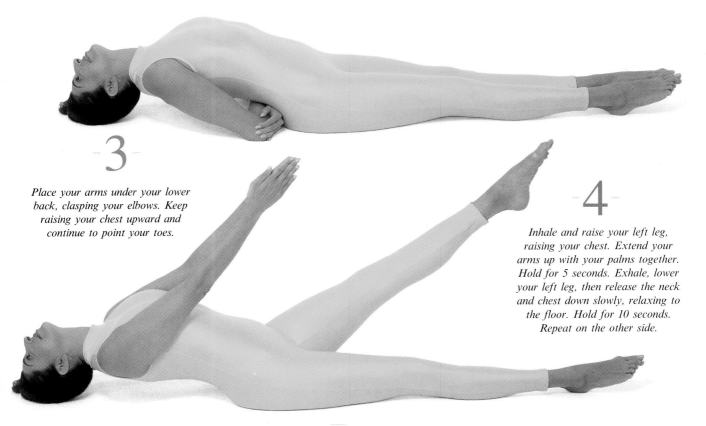

3

Place your arms under your lower back, clasping your elbows. Keep raising your chest upward and continue to point your toes.

4

Inhale and raise your left leg, raising your chest. Extend your arms up with your palms together. Hold for 5 seconds. Exhale, lower your left leg, then release the neck and chest down slowly, relaxing to the floor. Hold for 10 seconds. Repeat on the other side.

Back Bend

All back bends strengthen the spine and open out the chest cavity to improve deep breathing. The movement increases blood circulation and raises energy levels. Even though back bends are strenuous to do, it is very important to keep your face relaxed and free of tension throughout. You will feel exhilarated in Step 4 as your whole body, especially your arms and legs, is strengthened. The deep breathing technique will also give you a feeling of complete calm.

2

Inhale and sit up tall, stretching your arms upward in line with the side of your head. Stretch out your legs slightly, but keep your feet together. Breathe normally.

1

Lie flat on the floor and bring your knees up. Place your feet as close to your body as possible. Stretch both your arms out behind your head and breathe normally.

3

Keeping your feet flat on the floor, balance your arms behind you. Place your palms in opposite directions to your feet to support your body weight. Inhale and lift your buttocks, keeping an even line between your knees, hips and shoulders. Look up, exhale and breathe normally for 5 seconds.

4

Inhale, extend your legs and straighten your knees. Drop your head back and relax the neck and face. Keep pushing your hips upward. Breathing normally, hold for 5 seconds.

The Cobra

The Cobra strengthens and tones the lower back muscles. It alleviates back pain and prevents other common back ailments. The action of The Cobra tightens the buttock muscles and increases the intra-abdominal pressure which tones the uterus and ovaries. It also regulates the menstrual cycle and helps the thyroid and adrenal glands to work more effectively.

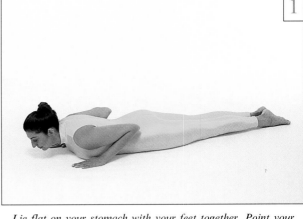

Lie flat on your stomach with your feet together. Point your toes, bend your arms close to your body, and place your palms flat under your shoulder blades. Point your chin downward.

Return to Step 1, but this time place your hands under the breastbone and point your elbows outward.

2

Inhale and raise your head off the floor. Place your hands on the floor with your elbows inward. Keep your chin up and make sure your hip bones stay on the floor. Breathe normally and hold for 10 seconds. On the last exhalation, slowly lower yourself to the floor and return to Step 1. Repeat.

4

Inhale, push down and lift your body off the floor. Look upward, keeping your shoulders down and your hips just off the floor. Breathing normally, hold for 10 seconds. On the last exhalation, slowly lower yourself and relax.

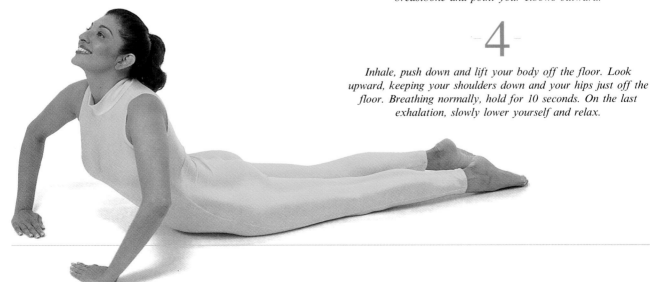

Back Lift

This exercise is rather strenuous to do and your body needs to be correctly aligned to achieve the right results. Not only does this type of lift tone the legs, buttocks, and stomach muscles, it also strengthens the lower back to enable you to sit and stand with perfect posture. Both your hip bones and shoulder blades should remain on the floor to stop you moving from side to side throughout the exercise. As a beginner you need not worry about the height of your leg lift, but as you gain strength and continue practicing, your hips will become more flexible and you will be able to lift your legs even higher.

Lie on the floor face down. Keep your back straight and place your arms by your sides, holding your hands as fists. Inhale and raise your left leg, keeping your hips square. Breathe normally and hold for 6 seconds. On the last exhalation slowly lower the leg, then inhale and repeat on the other side.

Inhale and raise your legs. Place your forehead on the floor. Keep lifting, breathing deeply, for as long as you can. On the last exhalation lower both legs. Repeat, then turn your head to one side and relax.

2

With your feet together, raise your hips slightly off the floor with your elbows resting under the hip bones. Keep your hands in fists, balanced under the thighs for support.

Cat Stretch

This is a wonderful body stretch to release tension trapped in the spine. It is excellent if you are very tired, as it invigorates the nervous system and helps calm the mind. If you are experiencing any back pain this is the best way to ease it. This is a relaxed pose, so you can hold it for as long as you wish. Inhale and exhale deeply to increase the calming effect.

1

Lie flat on the floor and bend your arms, keeping your hands under your shoulder blades. Point your toes and relax your elbows, but hold them close to your body.

2

Inhale deeply and push down on your palms so that you can lift your hips upward into a kneeling position just like a cat.

3

Exhale and stretch your hips back so that you sit on your heels. Straighten your elbows, stretching your arms out in front of you. Place your forehead on the floor. Breathe normally and relax.

Soles of Feet

This Soles of Feet movement opens up the hips and increases flexibility in the hip joints, knees and thighs. Rotating the legs outward helps to increase the body's suppleness and also improves overall posture and mobility of the spine. It is an ideal exercise to do in preparation for giving birth, but take care not to bounce or jerk the spine.

Sit up tall on the floor with your legs in front of you. Bring the soles of your feet together and reach forward to place your hands around your ankles.

Bring the heels closer into your body and sit upright. Relax your shoulders, then stretch up from the pelvis and open out the chest.

To increase the stretch of the hips, thighs and knees, place your elbows over the knees. Bend over, curving your spine and keeping your shoulders down. Inhale, and as you exhale push your knees to the floor. Breathe and relax into the stretch, slowly lowering your head to your feet.

Breathe and Relax

Stretching out the body is the best way to release any stress in your muscles. Combining stretching movements with deep breathing helps to calm and relax the nervous system. It also increases energy levels, flexibility and suppleness of the muscles, and gives a sense of physical and mental well-being. Never force your body through the exercise – use gentle movements, flowing into each position. You will soon appreciate the rejuvenating joy and challenge of deep stretching.

1

Sit on the floor with your legs wide apart. Flex your toes upward and try to push your knees down to the floor. Clasp your fingertips together in front of you.

2

Inhale, lean forward and stretch your arms out, keeping your hands up over your head. Turn your thighs outward to increase the stretch.

◆ *Don't force yourself
into the stretches for
this exercise, but as
you become more
supple, try pushing
yourself a little
further forward or
upward.*

4

*Exhale, drop your head back and
look up to your clasped palms. Do
not cave in at the chest or release
your lower back. Inhale again and
return to Step 3.*

3

*Continue to inhale and raise your arms up high over your
head. Sit as tall as you can and open out your chest, keeping
your shoulders down.*

5

Inhale and as you exhale stretch
over to the right, keeping your
spine straight. Breathe normally
and hold for 5 seconds. Inhale
and then return to Step 3.

6

Exhale and stretch over to the left. Try
to balance your head evenly between your
arms. Breathe normally and again hold
for 5 seconds. Inhale and return to Step 3.

7

Exhale as you relax forward onto the
floor. Keep your toes flexed and try to
place your forehead right on the floor.
Inhale and exhale deeply for 20 seconds
and relax into the stretch.

Pranayama

'Prana' is the Sanskrit word for energy and 'pranayama' is the yoga breathing technique that unblocks this flow in the body and balances the masculine and feminine energies. Breathing correctly from the diaphragm acts as a natural tranquilizer and calms the nervous system. Always breathe through the nose, and as you exhale you will find that your lung capacity is increased and that more oxygen reaches the bloodstream. This rejuvenates the blood cells and increases vitality.

1

Sit cross-legged on the floor, or on a chair with your lower back supported, in which case keep your knees together and your feet flat on the floor. Place your thumb and first finger together and turn your palms upward. Focus on your diaphragm, and try to keep one thought in your mind. Breathe deeply, holding the position for at least 60 seconds.

2

To release tension in the neck and shoulders, inhale and raise your shoulders to your ears. Then exhale and lower them again. Repeat 3 times.

3

Return to Step 1. Drop your chin into your chest. Inhale and begin a full head circle to the right. Roll your head slowly, gently twisting your neck.

4

Take your head over to the right side, keeping your shoulders square to maximize the stretch. Keep your chin level.

5

Continue to inhale and drop your head all the way back behind you. As you exhale, roll your head to the left and complete the circle. Repeat on the other side.

COURSE TWO

By now you have become familiar with the general style of yoga exercises and you have gained more flexibility, strength and stamina. You are now ready to twist your body in various ways, remembering, of course, to start with the Warm-Up (see page 16).

In Course 2 you will experience the energy flowing from one position to another. The muscles, joints and blood vessels will all be stretched, so that the blood is equally distributed to every part of the body and more energy flows into the relaxed muscles.

Try to hold the postures for longer with a calm and still mind. The only difference between a beginner and an intermediate student of yoga is the length of time a pose is held. This gives time for the mind to focus and the body to cleanse, purify and build the system.

Salute to the Sun

The Salute to the Sun is the classic warm-up exercise for all yoga practice. It increases the energy flow and improves circulation and muscle flexibility in the whole body. It also tones every muscle group, builds strength and stamina, and teaches you how to be graceful and well-poised. It is important to learn to move gracefully from one position to the next. Always breathe properly, because not only will your vitality level and energy increase, you will also feel rejuvenated and calm. While you practice the sequence, think of yourself as a dancer with total control over your body. As you become more supple, try to repeat the entire exercise up to 10 times on each side.

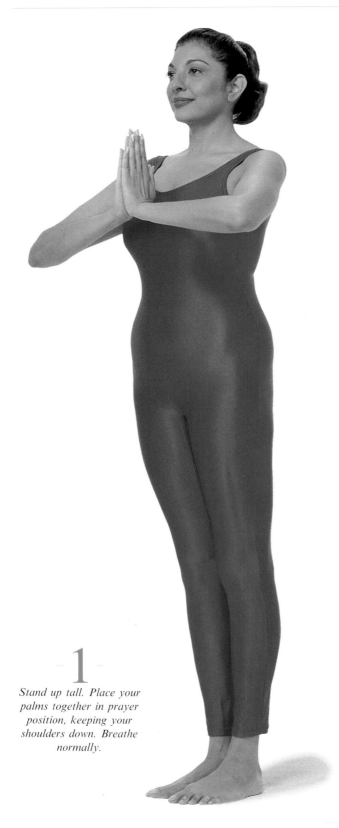

1

Stand up tall. Place your palms together in prayer position, keeping your shoulders down. Breathe normally.

2

Inhale and step to the right. Throw your arms back over your head and reach behind you. Push your hips forward, keeping your feet parallel and your toes pointed forward.

3

Exhale, step back with your feet together and bring your arms down. Stretch down to hold your ankles, pulling your forehead down to your knees.

4

Place your palms down on the floor in preparation for the next move. If you cannot keep your legs straight, bend your knees slightly.

5

Inhale and take your right leg back behind you. Balance on your toes and bend your left knee. This is the position a sprinter adopts when preparing for a race.

Leave your palms on the floor, inhale and stretch out both legs behind you. Keep your elbows straight and balance on your hands and feet. Keep your chin up and look forward.

6

Drop your right knee to the floor. Balance your weight at the top of your kneecap, but not on the kneecap itself, to prevent injury. Lift up your spine, raising your arms over your head with your palms together. Breathe normally and hold for a few seconds as you stretch.

Exhale, drop both your knees to the floor and look down to your hands.

Continue to exhale and sit back on your heels, stretching out your arms in front of you to release your spine.

Inhale again and dive forward like a snake, keeping your chin near the floor to make your spine flexible. Bend your elbows.

-7-

Release down to the position for Step 5, and drop your head with your chin toward your knee.

Continue inhaling and move forward, sliding out your chest and chin so that they are close to the floor.

Still inhaling, drop your hips down and straighten your arms into the Cobra pose. Curve your spine, turning your head up.

Exhale and return to Step 8, lifting your body up onto your toes again. Breathe normally.

15

Inhale and as you exhale, raise your hips, extending your spine. Keep your heels down on the floor and feel the stretch from your feet through your legs, spine, arms and into your fingers. This position is the Dog Pose. Breathe normally and hold for a few seconds.

16

Return to the Step 6 pose, inhale, but this time bring the right foot forward and the left leg back. Hold for a few seconds and breathe normally.

17

Exhale, stepping back with your feet together, and bring your arms forward to return to the Step 3 position.

18

Inhale and step to the left. Throw your arms out behind you and bend backward as far as possible as in Step 2.

19

Put your feet together as Step 1. Breathe deeply, holding for 5 seconds. Repeat, using the opposite leg in Steps 5 and 16.

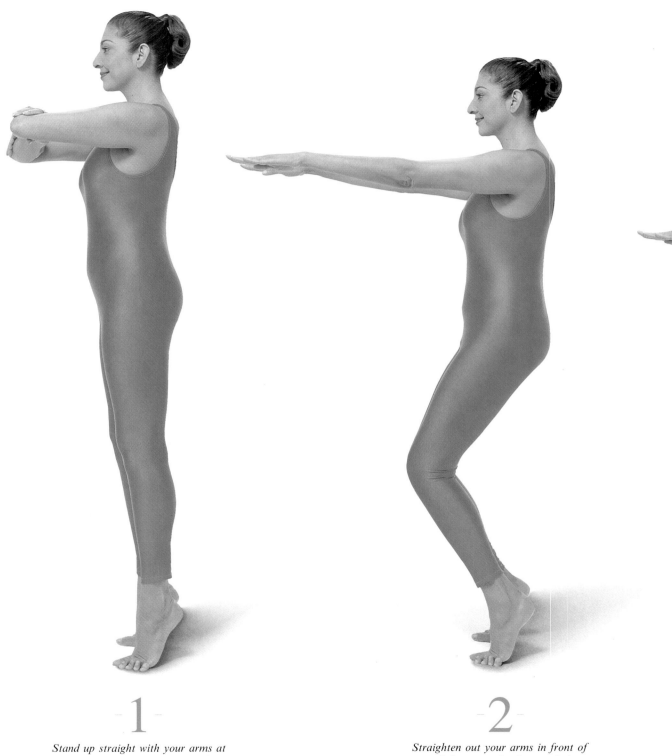

1

Stand up straight with your arms at your sides. Cross your arms in front of you and hold your elbows. Raise your heels and balance on your toes.

2

Straighten out your arms in front of you to help you maintain your balance. Bend your knees, keep your spine perfectly straight and try to hold still.

Knee Bends

These knee bend exercises build stamina and strength in the leg muscles as well as the abdominals. Balance is the key factor to doing them well, plus intense concentration. They help tone the spine as well as the calves, thighs and upper arms. The joints are also energized, which can prevent arthritis and rheumatism in the legs. These Knee Bends are grounding exercises which connect the earth's energy to the base of the spine. This energy then flows up the spine, increasing circulation and revitalizing your body.

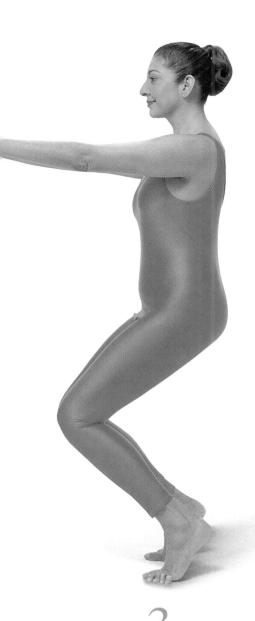

-3-

Bend your knees down further so that you feel the extra stretch in your thighs, and keep lifting your heels upward.

-4-

Bend right down to a squatting position. Your knees, thighs and hips should be in a line at a right angle to the floor. Breathe deeply and hold as long as you can.

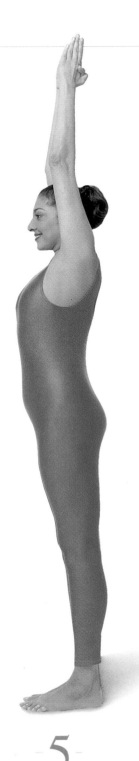

5

Stand up straight with your arms above your head. Cross your thumbs and put your palms together. Stretch your elbows, keeping your arms close to your head. Breathe normally.

6

Holding your upright posture, bend your knees but make sure that you keep your spine completely straight as you sink down toward the floor.

7

Inhale and take your hips back, making the movement from your tail bone. Adjust your weight to your heels and keep your back as straight as possible. Breathe normally and hold for 10 seconds.

The Eagle

The Eagle exercise focuses your mind so that you can concentrate on attention to detail. It grounds your energy and improves your balance. It can help to eliminate any cellulite and extra fat around the thighs, and also tones the leg, arm, and calf muscles. As you do the exercise, always keep your eyes fixed ahead on one spot to help you maintain your balance.

1

Stand up straight. Hold your left hand, facing upward, in front of your nose and stretch out your right arm. Focus on one spot straight ahead. Breathe normally.

2

Bend both your knees and wrap the right leg around the left. Try to wrap the right foot around the left ankle. The deeper you bend the easier it is to wind your leg.

3

Bring your right arm under your left, crossing them at the elbows, but keeping your shoulders down. Twist your right hand toward your left palm in front of your nose and press palms together. Keep your shoulders even, but press down to open the chest. Breathe normally, holding as long as possible. Repeat on the other side.

The Letter T

Performing the movements for Letter T is very challenging and builds up your strength and stamina. It is a powerful and dynamic stretch and is the only asana that should not be held longer than 10 seconds. It increases your pulse rate and you will feel your breath coming more quickly. The stretching also firms your buttocks and upper arms.

3

As you exhale stretch out from your tail bone in both directions. Keep stretching your spine forward and keep pointing your toes behind you until you reach a perfect Letter T. Deepen your breathing and hold the position for up to 10 seconds. Repeat on the other side.

Stand up straight with your feet together. Raise your arms above your head. Place your palms together and straighten your elbows. Push your elbows back behind your ears, keeping your shoulder blades down. Breathe normally.

Inhale deeply and point your right leg out behind you. Keep your right knee and your spine straight as you stretch out. Focus on one spot in front of you to keep your balance.

-Tips-

✦ It is important to breathe deeply from the diaphragm during the final position to increase your energy levels and vitality.

✦ Point your toes as much as possible. This will help to keep your knee and foot in a straight line.

✦ Keep pointing your toes and stretching your arms forward at the same time. Imagine you are a rubber band being stretched in opposite directions.

Leg Extension

This position gives you more
flexibility of the spine and builds
strength in your lower back and
legs. It opens the hips and makes
you slimmer around the hips. It is also
a difficult balancing exercise that focuses
your concentration. The final position is
quite hard to master, but don't get discouraged
if you can't get your forehead right down to
your knee.

1

*Stand up straight with your
feet together. Bend forward
and grasp your ankles.
Breathe normally.*

2

*Place both hands on the floor in front of you and
focus on one spot on the floor. Inhale and pull your
stomach muscles up, while raising your left
leg as high as possible. Keep the
knee straight and point your toes. Breathe
normally.*

3

Still concentrating hard, take your hands to your right ankle and keep lifting the kneecap up. Open your toes and grip the floor. Breathe normally.

4

Keep stretching your leg out behind you as you pull your head toward your knee. Try to hold for as long as possible, pointing your toes upward, then slowly return to an upright position. Repeat on the other side.

The Tower

This series of movements increases the strength in your legs and also makes your spine more flexible. It expands the chest, helping you to breathe more deeply and improving your lung capacity. The exercise also helps to relieve any stiffness in the neck and shoulders and make them more supple. At the end of The Tower, when your head is resting on your knee, the abdominal organs are toned and cleansed – this is because your deep breathing has pumped fresh oxygen into the blood, increasing the circulation and revitalizing and purifying them.

Stand upright with your feet about 1m (3ft) apart and your toes pointing forward. Take your arms up so that your palms face each other and straighten your elbows, keeping your shoulders down. Breathe normally.

Turn your left foot to a 90° angle, while moving the right foot slightly inward. The heel of the left foot should be in line with your right instep. Keep your head evenly balanced between your arms.

Bend your left leg so that your thigh is parallel to the floor. Throw your arms up and cross your thumbs with your palms together. Look upward and arch your spine. Breathe deeply and hold for 8 seconds.

4

Straighten your head between your arms and move your body forward with your weight on your left leg. Keep your leg, spine and arms in a straight line. Breathe deeply and hold for 8 seconds.

5

Relax down to the floor and place your hands on the floor. Drop your head to your knee. Keep breathing normally.

6

With your head still at your knee and with your palms on the floor, inhale and straighten the knee as much as possible. Breathe normally and hold for 8 seconds. Return to Step 1 and repeat on the other side.

Deep Lunge

The Deep Lunge exercises every muscle and tendon in the body. The intensity of the side stretch trims the thighs, hips and waistline, invigorates the internal organs and soothes the nerves. The position of the spine in relation to the hips helps to balance the endocrine system – the pituitary gland, thyroid, gonads and pancreas, all of which are glands that secrete hormones – as well as releasing toxins that build up in the system.

1

Adopt the Warrior pose (page 32), making sure your left leg makes a 90° angle and the back of your knee is in line with your heel. You can take the right leg further out to increase the lunge. Breathe normally.

2

Take your left hand down to your left ankle, turn your upper body and look over your right shoulder, twisting as much as possible. Place your right hand on the inner left thigh to increase the twist. Breathing deeply, hold for 8 seconds.

3

Place your left palm down on the floor and extend your right arm, elbow straight, close to your ear. Keep looking upward. Breathing deeply, hold for 8 seconds.

4

Inhale and raise your body, keeping your spine in the same position. Clasp your hands together over your head and stretch upward. Breathing deeply, hold for 8 seconds, then return to Step 1. Straighten the knee and repeat on the other side.

Side Lunge

This series of movements increases flexibility of the spine, improves balance and tones and cleanses the abdominal organs. You may feel dizzy or nauseous during the exercise, but this is a good sign – it means you are releasing toxins in the system. Just stop if you feel in any way uncomfortable and breathe deeply to regain your equilibrium. Always stretch from the tail bone and keep your hips and torso square to the side.

Exhale and, keeping your spine straight and your chin up, lower yourself to a 90° angle to the floor.

Still exhaling, bend and rest your forehead on your knee. Keep both legs straight – lift the muscles above the kneecaps to maintain balance. Breathing normally, hold for 6 seconds.

1

Follow feet positions in Steps 1 and 2 of Side Stretch (page 29). Place palms together behind your lower back or toward the mid-back. Push the elbows toward each other and open the chest. Look up and bend back as far as possible. Inhale deeply.

Bend your left knee and lunge forward. Drop your head down on the inner side of the knee. Breathe deeply and hold for 6 seconds.

Straighten your knee, relax your arms down and place your hands on the floor, palms down. Breathe deeply and hold for as long as you can.

Inhale and raise your body so that your back is flat, with your arms back and upward. Breathing normally, hold for 6 seconds.

-7-

Return to an upright position, take your feet and arms through the center as in Step 1 of Side Stretch and repeat on the other side.

Front Lunge

This exercise is beneficial both mentally and physically. Stretching forward from the hips calms and soothes the central system, lifts fatigue, refreshes the mind and invigorates the blood circulation. The flexibility of the hamstrings, hips and spine is improved and the leg muscles are toned. Make sure that you always stretch forward from the tail bone and hold your stomach muscles up. Keep your spine straight throughout the exercise and breathe deeply from the diaphragm in order to increase the relaxing effect.

Stand tall with your feet 1.2m (4ft) apart. Place your hands on your hips. Inhale and as you exhale move your torso forward to flat-back position, keeping your chin up.

-Tips-

+ *Pay attention to your breathing, and take care not to hold your breath.*

+ *Push your weight onto your heels and grip the floor with your toes in order to steady your balance.*

+ *Keep your fingertips together in Step 4.*

+ *Whenever you straighten your legs, lift the leg muscles above the kneecap, to avoid injury.*

Still exhaling, relax forward, placing your hands on the floor. Push your weight to your heels, raise your hips back, grip the floor with your toes; open your fingers and stretch your spine.

Walk your hands back and distribute your weight evenly between your heels and toes. Lift your chin and keep your back straight.

4

Inhale and raise your arms evenly on both sides. Keep your elbows straight and your fingertips together. Breathe deeply and hold for 6 seconds.

▶

Relax your arms and drop your forehead down toward the floor.
Breathe normally.

6

Inhale and clasp your hands around your ankles. Exhale and stretch your forehead down toward the floor. Breathe normally and hold for 6 seconds. Make sure your arms and legs are straight.

7

Bend your elbows and relax your knees. Push your palms down on the floor and prepare to jump into first position.

Inhale and jump. Breathe normally and balance on your toes. Steady yourself by placing your fingertips on the floor. Straighten the legs first, then the spine and stand in perfect posture.

Toe Balance

The Toe Balance is an excellent way to improve concentration and confidence. All balances give you a sense of achievement, even if you are only able to hold the position for a few seconds. The most important thing to remember is that balance is a natural state of the mind and body which is lost as a result of the stresses and strains of daily living. These balancing exercises are designed to bring harmony to your total being and correct bad alignment caused by poor posture. You will know immediately when you are in correct alignment because you will feel a sense of joy and elation. Remember when you are trying to balance that it helps to focus on an object directly in front of you. Think of yourself as being absolutely still like a statue.

Squat on the floor, balancing on your toes with your knees together. Place your fingertips on the floor for support and cross your left leg across your right thigh. Keep your torso upright and breathe normally.

Focusing your gaze on one point, lift your left foot off the floor. When you feel totally balanced, bring your palms together and hold the position for as long as possible. Keep trying until you master the balance. Repeat on the other side.

Spinal Twist

The Spinal Twist opens the hip area, increases flexibility of the spine and releases toxins from the adrenal glands. It also tones the abdominal organs, kidneys, and spleen, aids digestion and cures digestive disorders. This pose stimulates the blood circulation to the spine and relieves backache. Because the abdominal wall is being contracted the abdominal muscles are stretched on both sides. When you are in the final position you will feel invigorated and energized.

1

Sit on the floor with both legs stretched straight out in front of you. Flex your right foot and take your left leg into a half-lotus. Sit upright and try to bring your left knee down to the floor. Breathe normally.

2

Reach sideways toward your right foot, bend your elbow and clasp two fingers around the foot, extending your thumb. Twist your spine and look over your left shoulder. Take your left arm around the lower back and take hold of the toes of your left foot. Keep twisting and turn your torso upward. Breathe deeply and hold for 10 seconds.

3

Release your left arm and take it sideways over your head to touch the right thumb. Keep your head even between your arms. Breathing normally, hold for 10 seconds. Repeat on the other side.

Sitting Balance

The Sitting Balance is an excellent test for checking your alignment – you will be unable to carry out this exercise if your spine is not in the correct position. Imagine your spine to be a group of children's building blocks; if you do not place each block evenly on to the next the whole building will come tumbling down. By the same token, if you do not lift your spine upright you will keep rolling back down to the floor. Concentrate on your stomach muscles because it is equally important to pull them in at the same time as you lift your spine.

2

Still sitting upright, bring your legs up to form an exact right-angle with the body.

1

Sit upright and bring your knees up with your feet flat on the floor. Clasp your elbows under your knees. Keep your spine straight and breathe normally.

4

Shift your hands up your legs and take hold of your ankles. Pull your head toward your knees, keeping your spine straight and pulling your stomach muscles in. Breathe normally and hold for at least 5 seconds.

Straighten both legs up in front of you and hold the position absolutely still for at least 5 seconds, breathing normally.

The Plough

This is an all-body stretch that maximizes the flexibility of the spine and tones the leg and stomach muscles. The locking of the chin into the chest stimulates the thyroid gland, which regulates the metabolism and the hormonal levels in the body. Consequently, the Plough can help to cure an overactive or underactive thyroid and stabilize weight gain and irregular menstrual cycles. This inverted position unblocks energy, improves circulation and calms the nerves. Keep your breathing deep and even to achieve maximum benefits. Do not attempt inverted postures if you are pregnant or if you have a heavy menstrual period.

1

Lie flat on the floor with your arms to the sides, palms facing down. Inhale and, using your stomach muscles, bring your knees into your chest. Keep your shoulders down and relax the muscles in your face.

2

Exhale and throw your legs behind your head to the floor. Point your toes and straighten your knees. Keep stretching your legs and lock your chin into your chest. Breathe deeply.

3

To increase the stretch, tuck your toes under and clasp your hands together. Continue to breathe deeply.

Tips

♦ If keeping the knees straight is
difficult you can bend them
slightly to avoid back strain.

♦ If you find difficulty breathing
in the inverted position,
descend back down to the
floor, breathe deeply and
relax. Resume the position
when you feel ready.

To release the position, take both
arms and legs behind you and
place your toes into your palms.
Close your eyes, breathe deeply
and hold for 5 to 10 seconds.

4

Holding the same
position, inhale and raise
your right leg straight up.
Point the toes and keep
both knees straight.
Breathing normally, hold
the position for 5 seconds.
On an exhalation lower
the leg slowly and repeat
on the opposite leg.

6

To relax the spine drop your
knees to the floor, close to your
ears. Take your arms down in
front of you, palms facing down.
Hold for 5 to 10 seconds.

7

To begin the descent back, lift your knees off the floor and place them just above your face. Point your toes and concentrate on your spine. Breathe normally.

8

Focus on your stomach muscles and lower back and slowly straighten your legs behind you, keeping the top of your spine on the floor. Breathe normally.

9

Exhale and, moving very slowly and with concentration, roll your spine down, working from the top vertebrae down to the tail bone without missing any sections. Return the legs to a right angle and hold for a few seconds, breathing normally. On an exhalation, using your stomach muscles, slowly lower your legs without raising your spine. Relax and breathe normally.

The Wheel

The Wheel, Bow and Camel are intense back bends that invigorate the spine, alleviate back pain and increase the lung capacity. We rarely stretch backward and these positions release fear and bestow a positive outlook on life. All three asanas release energy in the body's cells, glands and organs. The Wheel also builds muscle tone in the legs, hips, shoulders, arms, wrists and hands. Holding the position will build body strength and give stamina to the spine and limbs.

Lie flat, knees bent and in line with your hips, and feet flat and as close to the buttocks as possible. Inhale and raise your buttocks as high as possible. Try to hold on to your ankles. Breathe normally. Lower down and repeat.

Keeping your feet in the same position, lift your hips and buttocks and take your arms over your head with palms facing downward. Push up and rest on the crown of your head. Breathe normally and hold for 5–10 seconds.

Lift as high as possible, balancing on your toes and hands. Straighten your elbows and, breathing normally, hold for as long as possible. Return to Step 2, lift your head toward your chest and lower your spine, one vertebra at a time, with your tail bone last.

The Bow

This exercise is called the Bow because of the beautiful bow shape that the spine creates. The back muscles and internal organs are massaged and the latter invigorated. Because of the position of the abdomen, this asana helps to cure digestive and bowel disorders such as gastroenteritis and constipation. It also stimulates the appetite, aids digestion and reduces fat along the stomach and middle of the back. As a result of the increased suppleness it gives to the spine every cell in the body is rejuvenated and revitalized, giving you renewed vitality and a more youthful appearance.

Lie on your stomach and lift your legs up behind you. Hold on to your ankles and point your toes. Place your chin and nose on the floor. Breathe normally.

2

Inhale and lift your body up in one movement. Balance on your hip bones and keep stretching upward, trying to get your head in line with your feet. Breathe deeply and hold for as long as you can.

The Camel

The Camel tones the entire spine as well as every muscle group in the body, building strength in the lower back and alleviating back ailments, especially sciatica and slipped discs. It is also a wonderful stretch for the face and neck – the increased circulation helps to prevent the signs of ageing. Every time you do this exercise, feel your body giving way into the stretch and relax and open the throat and chest; do not allow any weight into the thighs or leg muscles. Always push upward from the hips to increase the intensity of the back stretch and breathe deeply throughout. If you experience a sharp pain in the lower back, stop immediately and relax in Step 3. A dull pain means you are using muscles around the spine that need toning.

Kneel down, spine straight and hips directly above your knees. Hold on to your elbows behind your lower back. Inhale, push your hips forward and drop your head back. Breathe normally.

Continuing to push your hips forward, take your hands to your heels. Open your chest and throat and relax your face, neck and shoulders. Say 'Aah' in a clear tone to test that you are in the correct position. Breathe normally and hold for as long as possible.

To release the spine, reverse the position by relaxing your head down to the floor with your palms facing up. Breathe normally and repeat the exercise.

The Rabbit

The Rabbit allows fresh oxygen into the blood supply, which stimulates and invigorates the brain cells. The upside-down position of the head has a beneficial effect on the pituitary gland and thyroid. It wards off senility, clarifies the mind, regulates the metabolism and strengthens the immune system. It also has a calming effect on the nervous system. A preliminary exercise to the Head Stand (page 124), the Rabbit improves the elasticity and mobility of the spine.

2

Inhale and as you exhale curl your spine and place your forehead on the floor as close as you can to your knees. Breathe normally.

3

Roll on to the top of your head. Straighten your elbows and raise your hips. Breathe deeply and hold for 20 seconds. Return to Step 1 and repeat the exercise.

1

Kneel on the floor, toes tucked under your haunches. Clasp your hands to your heels and sit up tall. Breathe normally.

Eye Exercise

This exercise strengthens and tones the muscles in and around the eyes, increasing circulation and preventing wrinkles and fine lines from forming. It is also called the Clock because in doing it you visualize the numbers of a clock in clockwise and counter-clockwise fashion. Do not move your head but exaggerate the movement of your eyes. You may experience some strain but this is due to weak eye muscles; rub your hands together to make them warm and then cup your eyes to rest them. The shoulder stretch is optional, but it is a good companion to the eye stretch.

-2-

Keeping your chin level, look up at the number 12 of an imaginary clock. Focusing on each number, move your eyes clockwise, then repeat counter-clockwise. Repeat the exercise on the other side.

-1-

Kneel on the floor, tucking your toes under. Take your right arm over your right shoulder, placing your palm face down between your shoulder blades. Take your left arm around and clasp your hands together.

Pranayama

Pranayama are breath control exercises that allow the breath to flow smoothly through the seven chakra centers and unblock any negative energies. They also force the mind into intense concentration and traditionally are preliminary techniques to train the mind for meditation. Alternative nostril breathing balances the masculine and feminine energies which each of us has regardless of gender. It is vital for total mental and physical health to harmonize and balance these forces. The right nostril is the masculine side, so the breath will be deeper, louder and stronger; the left or feminine side will be soft, cool and quiet. As you inhale and exhale, concentrate on this and experience the difference between the breaths.

Sit cross-legged or in lotus or half lotus position, your spine upright. Touch your left thumb and first finger together and fold the three middle fingers of your right hand into your palm, extending your thumb and little finger.

Take your right hand to your nose and block the left nostril with your little finger. Inhale and exhale deeply through the right nostril only. Continue for 10 breaths.

Block the right nostril with your thumb and breathe for 10 seconds. Repeat the exercise 3 times on each side. Finish by breathing through both nostrils as in Step 1.

COURSE THREE

Course 3 is physically and mentally challenging and, as always, it is very important to warm up first. For you to enjoy these asanas you will need to have mastered the art of balance. At this level you will be totally centered and your approach to the asanas will be meditative. The exercises are dynamic and you will feel the energy flow from your toes through to your fingertips. Remember that the more energy you use, the more energy you will gain.

There is never a peak of perfection in any posture. Every time you begin an asana, challenge yourself to stretch further and hold the position for longer than the previous time.

Set goals for yourself and tell yourself that you definitely can and will improve.

Feel the stress leave your body as you twist and stretch. Think of your mind as the intelligent driver of a perfect automobile. You are the master of your soul and destiny and your yoga will take you to a new realm of calm, joy and contentment.

Vinyasa

Vinyasas are a series of different movements done in an active and dynamic style. Their function is to increase the stamina and strength of the body and to have an aerobic effect on the heart. Consequently, they are meant to be strenuous in nature and I have specifically designed this series to challenge your skill and to encourage you to develop grace through dynamic movement. Pay attention to the exact postures and do not rush. Breathe deeply and evenly through each of the positions.

1

Stand tall with your feet in second position directly under your hips and your knees bent. Inhale and throw your arms forward in parallel position.

2

Exhale, place your hands on the floor and jump, taking your feet out behind you. Stretch your spine and keep your legs and arms straight. Breathe normally.

3

Inhale, lift your heels and rise onto your toes. Change your foot position and balance on the front of your toes. Lower your hips toward the floor and raise your spine. Keep your shoulders down and look up. Breathe normally.

5

Exhale and place your left arm back down to the floor and swing your hips toward the floor. Tuck your toes under and point both hands forward and under the shoulder blades. Breathe normally.

4

Keeping your body in a straight line, turn your right hand to the front and your legs and feet together to the side. Raise your hips to maintain the straight line and raise your left arm, palm facing forward. Breathe deeply and hold for a few seconds.

6

Drop to your knees and begin to relax the spine. Breathe deeply.

7

Take your hips all the way back to your heels. Stretch your arms out in front of you. Breathe deeply and relax for a few moments.

8

Keeping your hands in the same position, inhale and dive down, leading with your chin and moving your chest smoothly as close to the floor as possible.

9

Exhale, sweep the spine forward and come up into the Cobra pose. Breathe normally.

10

Inhale and return to the one-arm balance as in Step 4, but on the other side. Make sure your alignment is correct. Breathe normally and try to hold still for as long as you can.

11

Exhale and return to Step 5. Inhale and return to Step 2. Breathing normally, increase the stretch.

12

Inhale and raise your right leg in a straight line behind you. Point the toes, hold, and breathe deeply. Repeat on the other leg.

13

Walk your hands back to your feet. Bend your knees and balance on your toes. Straighten your spine and hold for a few seconds. Return to standing position and repeat the entire series.

Half Lotus

This exercise is a wonderful challenge because it combines balance with concentration. In all difficult standing postures it is essential to keep the weight-bearing leg absolutely still when progressing through the various movements. Make sure the leg is pulled up as high as possible by gripping the floor with your toes and lifting the muscle above the kneecap.

1

Stand up straight. Lift your right foot up and bring your heel as close as possible to the left hipbone. Breathe normally.

2

Push your right foot against your left leg and balance your weight on your left leg.

3

Bring the palms together to help focus your attention. Make sure your shoulders are down and your face is relaxed.

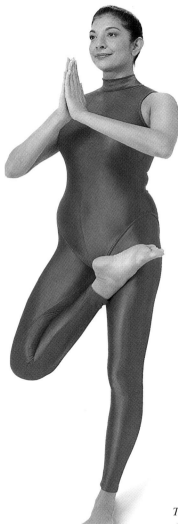

5

Release the foot and return to center position. Change legs and repeat on the other side.

4

Twist to the right and look over your right shoulder if you can. Having reached your maximum stretch, take your right hand around the back and reach for the right foot. Breathe normally and hold for a few moments.

Side Leg Stretch

This exercise looks simple but is in fact quite challenging. All the muscles in the legs are being toned and strengthened and suppleness is increased as you stretch to the side. The most important thing to remember is to keep the hips square. Open your chest without altering your posture and keep lifting as tall as you can. This position creates a positive attitude and the balance gives you steadiness and poise.

Tips

+ *In all balancing exercises, keep your eyes focused on one spot as this helps to center your body and focus your mind.*

+ *If your ankle wavers from side to side during this exercise, grip the floor with your toes.*

+ *Do not collapse your spine forward when you clasp your toes in Step 2.*

+ *If you cannot stretch your leg completely in Step 3, bend your knee.*

-1-

Stand up straight. Imagine a string is pulling you up from the top of the head to straighten your spine further. Put your left hand on your waist and use your right hand to lift your right leg up to the inner left thigh. Breathe normally.

3

Inhale, extend your right leg out from the knee and straighten your spine, taking care not to swivel your hips. Breathe normally and hold for as long as you can. Repeat on the other side.

2

Lean to the right, taking care not to twist your spine. Open your chest, clasp the two first fingers of your right hand around your big toe and extend the thumb. Breathe normally.

Head to Knee

This is the most difficult of the standing postures but it is well worth persevering with; not only does it build strength and stamina, it energizes the body, increases the flexibility of the spine and tones the lower region of the spine and the nerves connected to the legs. It also tones every muscle in the body, massages the internal organs and cures gastric problems. This is an excellent exercise for those who suffer from arthritis of the knees. It is important to hold the position for a length of time to allow the energy to flow in a circular motion throughout the system to improve circulation.

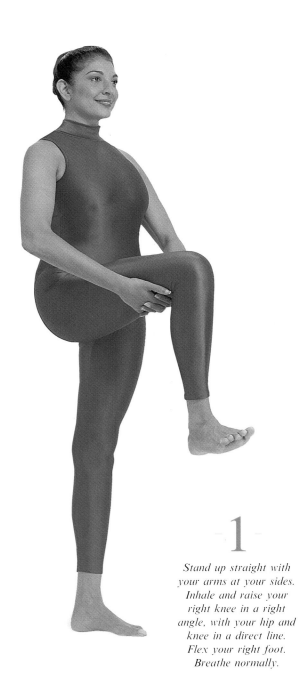

1

Stand up straight with your arms at your sides. Inhale and raise your right knee in a right angle, with your hip and knee in a direct line. Flex your right foot. Breathe normally.

2

Keeping your knee in a direct line with your hip, take hold of your right foot and pull it back. Keep your spine straight and focus your eyes on one spot to help you balance.

3

Inhale and extend the leg out directly in front of you. Keep your hips square and both knees straight. Breathe deeply and hold for 10 seconds.

4

Inhale and shift your weight to your heel. Do not bend the standing knee. Flex your foot harder, pull your stomach in, bend your elbows and stretch forward from the base of your spine, keeping your spine straight. Drop your forehead down to your knee and hold for as long as possible, breathing deeply. Repeat on the other side.

Standing Bow

This graceful exercise, called the Standing Bow because of the curve of the spine, will give you a sense of elation and power when you hold the pose as long as possible. The energy is continuously flowing in a circular pattern and as you increase the stretch your breathing pattern will quicken. Breathe deeply from the diaphragm to increase energy levels. This exercise will rejuvenate your spine and give you a sense of joy. Your circulation will be greatly improved and your whole body toned.

1

Stand up straight with your arms at your sides. Take your right leg behind you and hold the inner side of your foot. Straighten your elbow.

2

Take your left arm up close to your ear. Keep both shoulders down and look straight ahead. Breathe normally and steady your balance.

4

Move your upper body forward smoothly and keep stretching your back leg upward. Breathe deeply. Imagine you are an elastic band and continue to stretch until the toe of your raised leg is directly above the top of your head, or until your energy snaps and releases. Repeat on the other side.

3

Inhale, lift the right leg up from the hip as high as possible and then extend the left arm forward. Breathing normally, stretch in opposite directions.

Half Moon

This asana conveys harmony, balance, poise and power. It will give you a sense of achievement to flow into the final pose gracefully, without jerking. Before you begin the exercise, imagine yourself in the final position and feel as if you are a dancer as you move from one step to the next. The Half Moon also strengthens and tones the leg muscles and improves concentration.

Stand in a wide second position with arms outstretched to the sides.

Tips

+ *If the alignment of your spine and limbs are not perfect in Step 4, you will not be able to raise your leg with ease.*

+ *Looking over your shoulder in the final position is an ultimate challenge because it means you are in perfect balance. As you turn your head, do not jerk or move the body. Look immediately to one point and steady your gaze – otherwise you will tumble down.*

+ *Challenge yourself by trying to hold the final position for longer each time.*

Breathing normally, turn your left foot to the left at a 90° angle. Make sure your left heel is in a direct line with the instep of the right foot. Stretch from the base of the spine to the left side.

Bend your left knee, take your right hand to your waist and place your left hand on the floor. Look straight ahead and steady your balance. Breathe normally.

Focus on one spot on the floor. Inhale as you straighten your left knee and raise your right leg off the floor. Breathing normally, hold as long as possible; look over your right shoulder if you can. Repeat on the other side.

Lunge
with Balance

This exercise strengthens and tones all the muscles of the legs, stomach and arms. It builds stamina and suppleness of the spine. The position of the back stimulates the heartbeat and, with the increased oxygen pumped to the lungs, rejuvenates and energizes the entire body. The aim is to increase the mind control over the body while focusing attention and concentration on the physical. It needs tremendous skill to master this exercise, so do not become discouraged if it takes some time to learn. When you are in this pose it gives you a sense of harmony, balance, poise and power. It is especially recommended for runners and dancers as it brings vigor, agility and good carriage.

Stand in a wide second position with your feet 1m (3ft) apart. Throw your arms up with your elbows straight and palms facing each other.

Turn your right foot to the right in a 90° angle to the left foot. Make sure the right heel is in line with the instep of the left foot. Breathe normally.

Lunge with your right leg and create a straight line from the back of the knee to the heel. You might need to adjust your left leg by taking it back further.

Take your body forward from the lower back so that your spine, arms and left leg are in an exact straight line. Focus your gaze on one spot on the floor. Inhale and exhale deeply.

Inhale as you move your body forward and lift your left leg behind you. Flex the foot and try to keep parallel to the floor. Breathe deeply and hold as long as possible. Repeat on the other side.

Lunge with Back Twist

This, a variation of the previous exercise, calls for skill and a lot of determination. Pay special attention to the exact positioning of limbs, hands and feet. This is a powerful stretch, combining intense concentration with balance, suppleness, strength and stamina. Not only does it invigorate the internal organs, its deep twist releases toxins. If you feel sick and weak when you first begin this pose it means that your body is working to purify your system. Do not attempt Steps 4–7 until you have perfected Step 3.

1

Begin the pose as in Step 1 of previous exercise but with the arms outstretched to the sides. Change your foot positions as instructed in Step 2 of previous exercise and lunge to the right but do not twist the torso. Breathe normally.

-2-

Turn your whole body toward your right leg and place the fingertips of both hands on either side of the foot. Extend your left leg and balance on your toes.

-3-

Hook your left arm over the outer side of your right knee. Twist your torso to the right, pushing your elbow against your knee to increase the stretch. Both palms should be facing to the right. Breathing normally, hold for 10 seconds.

▶

4

Place your left hand on the floor directly in line with your right foot. Place your right hand on your waist.

5

Straighten your right leg and shift your weight to your right foot in preparation for the next step.

Inhale and raise your left leg. Breathe normally and find your balance.

When you are totally balanced, look over your right shoulder and increase the twist. Breathe normally and hold for as long as possible. Repeat on the other side.

Ultimate Twist

These two twists are classic positions to increase circulation in the spine and the abdominal organs, especially the liver and spleen. Twists cleanse and purify the system and are essential to the digestive system. Elimination is regulated, the kidneys are toned, and the blood circulation releases toxins that build up in the internal organs. When you are practicing twists you will find that every time you begin the pose it will be a different experience. As the flexibility of your spine increases you will be able to twist even further. Sluggishness will be replaced by higher energy levels and you will experience a feeling of youthfulness.

Sit with knees together and feet flat on the ground. Place your right elbow on the outside of your left knee and put your left hand on the floor in the opposite direction to your feet. Push against your knee and look over your left shoulder. Keeping your chin level and breathing normally, continue to stretch around. Hold for as long as you can. Repeat on the other side.

Sit with left leg over right leg. Take your right hand to the left knee and twist, looking as far over your left shoulder as possible. Place your left hand on the floor in line with your left leg. Breathe normally and continue to twist. Repeat on the other side.

Leg Pull

The Leg Pull increases the flexibility of the hamstrings and tones muscle in the knees and legs. It also tones the spine and massages the abdominal wall; blood flows around the navel and rejuvenates the genital organs. Never lift the knee that is resting on the floor – if there is too much of a pull on the kneecap do not extend your chin all the way to your knee.

1

Sit with both legs extended in front. Bend your left knee and bring your heel to your hip. Place your fingertips on the floor on either side of your body. Breathe normally.

2

Bend your right knee and clasp your first two fingers around your big toe. Flex your thumb and right foot and prepare for the stretch.

3

Keeping your spine straight, inhale and stretch the leg up in front of you. Hold your ankle and pull your leg towards you. Breathing slowly and evenly, hold for 20 seconds. If you can, place your chin and forehead to the leg. Repeat on the other side.

Total Stretch

This stretch is very controversial – some people find it excruciating, while others feel it to be the most marvelous of all the classic stretches. The truth is that the more flexible you are the easier the pose. It stretches every muscle in the thighs, knees and ankles, as well the entire spine. If you feel any pain in your back, place a pillow under the small of the back and open your chest. If you feel your knees are strained place a small pillow under the back of your knees. The most important thing to remember is to relax in the position. Breathe deeply and evenly and feel the chest and hips open.

Sit upright and bring your knees together. Spread your feet and rest them either side of your hips, with your buttocks on the floor. Place your palms facing forward on your feet.

Drop your body back down, taking your weight on your elbows, and feel the stretch in your legs and abdomen.

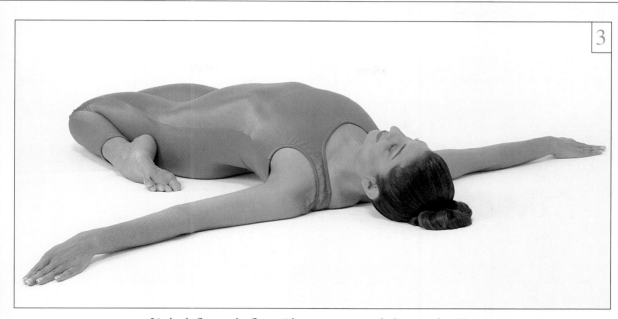

Lie back flat on the floor with your arms stretched out to the sides.

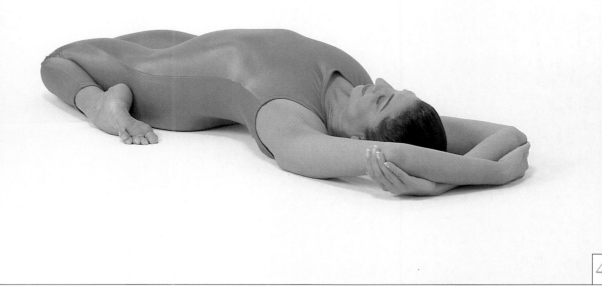

Clasp your elbows. Continue to breathe deeply and relax the entire body and mind. Try to hold this position for as long as possible – with practise you will be able to sustain it for 10–15 minutes.

Shoulder Stand

This is one of the most important asanas in classical yoga. Its benefits are many, the most important being that it stimulates and regulates the thyroid and parathyroid glands. Because of the chinlock, menstrual cycles regularize and weight remains stable. Healthy blood flows through the neck and chest, curing respiratory ailments and preventing sinus troubles and colds. Daily practice of this exercise cleanses the bowels and eliminates toxins.

-2-

Exhale and raise your legs to a 90° angle with your body, pointing your toes.

-3-

Inhale and take your legs over your head into the Plough position. Inhale and exhale.

-1-

Lie flat on the floor with your arms at your sides. Inhale and bring your knees into your chest.

5

*Bend your knees and
bring the soles of
your feet together.*

4

*Inhale and raise both legs as
high as possible – the aim is to
straighten the spine completely.
Lock your chin, point your toes
and place your hands in the
small of your back to support
your spine. Hold for 30 seconds,
breathing normally.*

▶

6

Straighten both legs behind you. Tuck your toes under, and breathing deeply, walk both feet to the right side of your head.

7

Drop both knees as close to your right ear as possible. Straighten both legs and walk your feet to the left, then drop your knees as close to your left ear as possible.

8

Bring both legs directly behind your head. Point your toes. Inhale and raise both legs directly parallel to the floor. Breathe normally.

9

Bend both knees and change the position of your hands, so your thumbs are on your tail bone and your fingers are on your waist.

10

Straighten your spine and split your legs, creating a 90° angle with your left leg. Repeat on the other side.

- 11 -

*Return to the classic
Shoulder Stand and
hold for 10 seconds.*

- 12 -

*Bend your right leg and
place the outer side of your
foot against your left thigh
just above your knee.*

14

Return to the classic Shoulder Stand and hold for 10 seconds.

13

Bring your right heel toward your left hipbone. Push the knee back so it is square with the left hip. Return to Step 11 and repeat 12 and 13 on the other side.

17

Twist the entire spine to the left. Return to center and rotate to the right side.

16

Push both hips back so they are square.

15

Begin the lotus position. Bend your right leg and with your left hand pull the right foot in as close to the left hipbone as possible. Repeat on the other side.

18

Return to the classic Shoulder Stand. Hold for 5-10 seconds.

19

Repeat Step 10 but extend the right leg. Point the toes of both feet.

20

Drop your left foot to the floor and point your right leg upward.

21

Bend your right knee and place both feet on the floor. Raise your hips as high as possible. Breathe normally.

22

Take your hands down to the floor and continue to raise your hips.

23

Exhale slowly and, working from the top of the spine, slowly lower one vertebra at a time until your spine is completely flat on the floor.

24

Relax your legs down to the floor and release your spine into the deep relaxation or Dead Man's pose. Relax for 5 minutes.

Head Stand

The Head Stand is called the king of all yoga asanas because it stimulates the pituitary and pineal glands. It is the gland that controls the brain, the seat of all wisdom, intelligence, discrimination and reasoning power. Without a healthy brain you cannot function. The inverted position of the Head Stand allows the blood to flow freely to the brain and feeds the brain cells with fresh oxygen. It gives you clarity of mind and wards off senility as you age. The brain also controls the entire nervous system and during the practice of the Head Stand all the nerves and cells are being rejuvenated. Health and vitality are restored and when you practice it on a regular basis you will develop the body, discipline the mind and broaden the spirit.

1

Kneel on the floor. Interlock your fingers, cross your thumbs and place your arms on the floor. Breathe normally.

2

Making sure your elbows are directly under your shoulder blades, place the top of your head down on the floor just in front of your hands.

3

Tuck your toes under and spring up onto your toes with your legs straight. Walk your feet toward your head until your spine is straight.

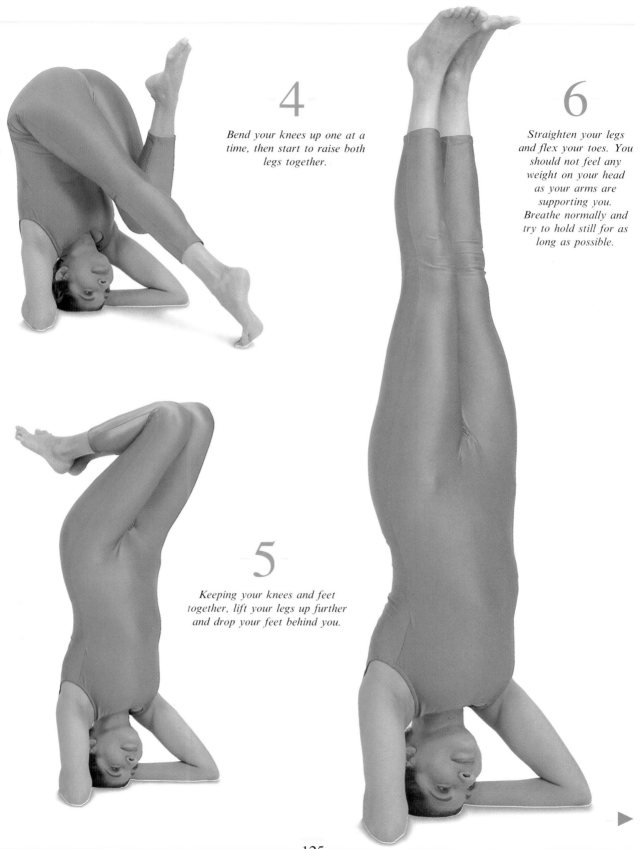

4

Bend your knees up one at a time, then start to raise both legs together.

5

Keeping your knees and feet together, lift your legs up further and drop your feet behind you.

6

Straighten your legs and flex your toes. You should not feel any weight on your head as your arms are supporting you. Breathe normally and try to hold still for as long as possible.

7

Open your legs to second position, keeping your feet flexed. Hold for 10 seconds.

8

Bend your knees at a right angle.

9

Slowly bring your knees forward, curving your spine, and return to the floor. Stay in this position for 10 seconds. If you come up suddenly you will feel dizzy.

Uddiyana

In Sanskrit, 'Uddiyana' means 'flying up'. In this exercise the air is drawn up from the lower abdomen and moves under the ribcage toward the head. This movement tones the abdominal organs, increases the gastric juices and eliminates toxins in the digestive tract. It is a wonderful way to exercise the muscles of the stomach, thereby making it flatter.

Kneel down on all fours. Keep your spine straight and place your hands and feet in a direct line. Inhale through your nose and exhale through your mouth until all the breath is out of your lungs.

Pull the stomach muscles up and curve your spine slightly. Without taking a breath, contract and release the muscles to massage the internal organs. When you tire, inhale and exhale normally for a few breaths. Repeat the whole exercise up to 20 times.

Acknowledgements

Executive Editor	Sian Facer
Art Director	Keith Martin
Design	Martin Topping
Editors	Jane McIntosh
	Mary Lambert
	Diana Vowles
Production	Melanie Frantz
	Candida Lane
Photography	John Adriaan
Hair and Make-up	Leslie Sayles
Director of Photography	Jon Acevski